FROM THE KITCHENS OF

HEALTHY✻CHOICE®

FOODS

GRILLING *Etc.*

MEALS FOR LIFE™

D1515998

CY DeCOSSE

INCORPORATED

A COWLES MAGAZINES COMPANY

CY DECOSSE INCORPORATED
A COWLES MAGAZINES COMPANY

Chairman/CEO: Bruce Barnet
Chairman Emeritus: Cy DeCosse
President/COO: Nino Tarantino
Executive V.P./Editor-in-Chief:
   William B. Jones

Healthy Choice© is a registered trademark of ConAgra Inc.
used under license by Cy DeCosse Incorporated.

Printed on American paper by:
Quebecor Graphics (0196)
Copyright © 1996
Cy DeCosse Incorporated
5900 Green Oak Drive
Minnetonka, Minnesota 55343
1-800-328-3895
All rights reserved
Printed in U.S.A.

Library of Congress Cataloging-in-Publication Data

Grilling etc.
    p. cm. -- (Meals for life™)
    Includes index.
    ISBN 0-86573-976-5
    1. Barbecue cookery. I. Cy DeCosse Incorporated.
    II. Series.
TX840.B3G7493   1996
641.5'784--dc20   95-38930

Table of Contents

Grilling Etc. gives you a new slant on meal preparation. The book not only focuses on a favorite cooking technique – grilling – it provides you with menu suggestions and extra recipes that help bring out the best in your grilled fare.

Etc. means that this book contains more than just recipes for the grill. Broiling, grilling's indoor counterpart, is also a featured cooking technique. Many of the broiling recipes include tips for grilling, so you can choose the technique you prefer. In addition, there are salad and side-dish recipes to complement the main-dish grilled and broiled recipes.

Menu suggestions appear with every recipe to aid in meal planning. These suggestions include the recipes from this book as well as simple complementary dishes designed to be prepared ahead of time or while your entrée is on the grill or under the broiler.

Menu suggestions focus only on the main components of the meal. Beverages and dessert ideas are not included. Balance the menus with fresh fruit and vegetables, low-fat milk, and breads. Choose low-fat, refreshing desserts like fruit, sorbet or angel food cake with a little chocolate sauce.

Grilling

There are many types of grills available. Charcoal grills cook food over a bed of hot charcoal briquettes, which impart a distinct smoky flavor to foods. Heat is regulated by adjusting air vents in the grill bottom and lid.

To prepare a charcoal grill, pile briquettes in a tight mound and light, using lighter fluid, an electric starter or a charcoal chimney. When a layer of white ash forms, spread coals about 1 inch beyond the cooking area for direct-heat cooking.

In direct-heat cooking, food is cooked directly over the coals. For indirect cooking, food is cooked over a drip pan, which is surrounded by coals.

Equipment

(1) foil; **(2)** nonstick vegetable cooking spray; **(3)** broiler pan with rack; **(4)** long-handled tongs, **(5)** basting brush and **(6)** spatula; **(7)** electric charcoal starter; **(8)** charcoal chimney; **(9)** lighter fluid; **(10)** charcoal briquettes

To judge the heat of the coals, hold the palm of your hand 6 to 8 inches above them. If you can hold it there for 2 to 4 seconds, the heat is high; 5 to 7 seconds, medium; 8 to 10, low.

Gas grills cook food over a bed of hot lava rocks. Temperature is controlled by regulating the gas flow. Indoor gills, either stove-top models or those built into a range, are also available. Follow the manufacturer's instructions for use with all these grills.

Broiling

Broiling is a cooking technique similar to grilling, in that food is cooked directly by a high heat source. Food is first placed on a broiler pan, baking sheet or baking dish that can endure high heat. The surface of the food is positioned anywhere from 3 to 6 inches from the heat source by placing it at the highest rack position in the oven.

Since food cooks quickly under high heat, it must be watched carefully to prevent burning. Marinating foods prior to broiling, or basting them while they broil, keeps them from drying out.

Broiler pans or baking sheets should be sprayed with nonstick vegetable cooking spray before food is placed on them, to prevent sticking. For easy cleanup, line the pan and rack with foil before spraying. Cut slits in the foil on the rack to allow for drainage.

Preheat the broiler before use. Do not preheat the pan, or the food may stick. When broiling in a gas stove, you may close the door, but leave the door ajar on an electric oven; otherwise, the thermostat will shut off the heating element.

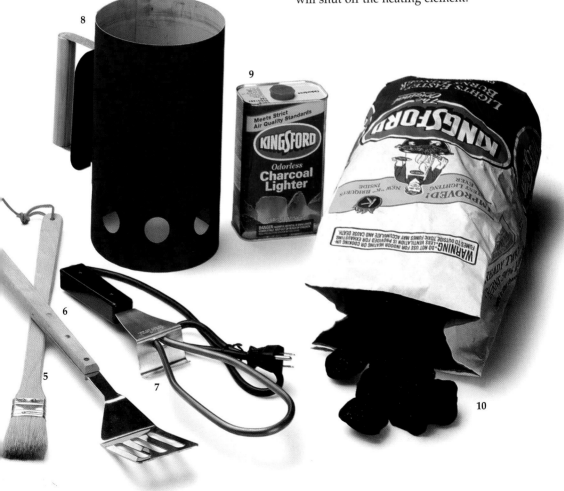

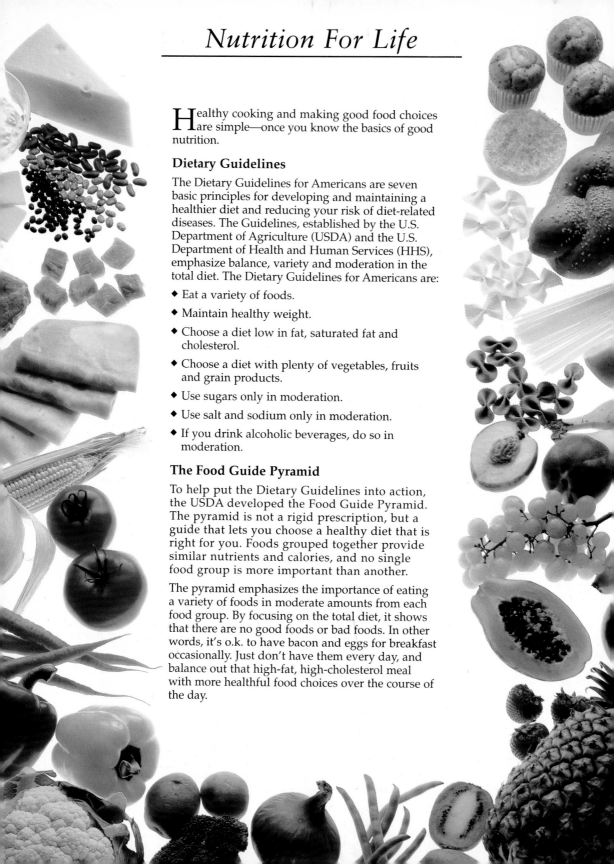

Nutrition For Life

Healthy cooking and making good food choices are simple—once you know the basics of good nutrition.

Dietary Guidelines

The Dietary Guidelines for Americans are seven basic principles for developing and maintaining a healthier diet and reducing your risk of diet-related diseases. The Guidelines, established by the U.S. Department of Agriculture (USDA) and the U.S. Department of Health and Human Services (HHS), emphasize balance, variety and moderation in the total diet. The Dietary Guidelines for Americans are:

- Eat a variety of foods.
- Maintain healthy weight.
- Choose a diet low in fat, saturated fat and cholesterol.
- Choose a diet with plenty of vegetables, fruits and grain products.
- Use sugars only in moderation.
- Use salt and sodium only in moderation.
- If you drink alcoholic beverages, do so in moderation.

The Food Guide Pyramid

To help put the Dietary Guidelines into action, the USDA developed the Food Guide Pyramid. The pyramid is not a rigid prescription, but a guide that lets you choose a healthy diet that is right for you. Foods grouped together provide similar nutrients and calories, and no single food group is more important than another.

The pyramid emphasizes the importance of eating a variety of foods in moderate amounts from each food group. By focusing on the total diet, it shows that there are no good foods or bad foods. In other words, it's o.k. to have bacon and eggs for breakfast occasionally. Just don't have them every day, and balance out that high-fat, high-cholesterol meal with more healthful food choices over the course of the day.

The Food Guide Pyramid

Fats, Oils & Sweets
Use sparingly

Milk, Yogurt & Cheese Group
2-3 Servings per day

Meat, Poultry, Fish, Dry Beans, Eggs & Nuts Group
2-3 Servings per day

Vegetable Group
3-5 Servings per day

Fruit Group
2-4 Servings per day

Bread, Cereal, Rice & Pasta Group
6-11 Servings per day

Reading the Pyramid

It's easy to follow the Food Guide Pyramid.

The bottom of the pyramid shows complex carbohydrates—the bread, cereal, rice and pasta group—at 6-11 servings a day. This group should be the foundation of a healthy diet.

The second level is made up of fruits and vegetables. We need to eat 3-5 servings of vegetables and 2-4 servings of fruit each day.

The third level is divided equally between milk, yogurt and cheese (2-3 servings a day) and meat, poultry, fish, beans, eggs and nuts (2-3 servings a day).

Most supermarkets now carry skim or low-fat milk and buttermilk; low-fat or nonfat yogurt, cottage cheese or ricotta cheese; and other low-fat cheeses.

A large variety of lean cuts of meat is also available in most stores. The leanest cuts of beef are the round, loin, sirloin and chuck arm. Pork tenderloin, center loin or lean ham, and all cuts of veal, except ground veal, are relatively lean. For lamb, the leanest cuts are the leg, loin and foreshanks. Chicken and turkey with the skin removed and most fish are lean meat choices.

The tip of the pyramid shows fats, oils and sweets. These include foods such as salad dressings, cream, butter, margarine, sugars, soft drinks and candies. Use them sparingly.

Build a diet of good food choices based on complex carbohydrates, and limit your intake of high-fat foods. The recipes in this book make it easy to fit nutritious meals into a busy schedule. And you don't have to choose between good taste and good nutrition. You can have them both.

Balancing Your Diet

The number of servings per day that is right for you depends on the amount of calories you need to maintain your best weight. The USDA recommends the following calorie levels per day: 1600 calories for many sedentary women and some older adults; 2200 calories for most children, teenage girls, active women and many sedentary men; and 2800 calories for teenage boys, many active men and some very active women. Each person's body is different, however, and you may need more or less depending on your age, sex, size, activity level and medical condition.

For example, if your calorie intake level is in the lower range, choose the smaller number of servings in each food group. Or, if you are very active, choose the larger number of servings in each group.

Serving Sizes

What counts as a serving?

You may be surprised. Use this chart to determine how your food intake compares to servings on the pyramid.

For combination foods, use your best judgment in estimating which food groups they fall into. For example, a large serving of pasta with tomato sauce and cheese could count in the bread group, the vegetable group and the milk group.

Milk, Yogurt & Cheese Group

2 ounces processed cheese, preferably reduced fat

1 cup low-fat milk or yogurt

1½ ounces natural cheese, preferably reduced fat

Meat, Poultry & Fish Group

½ cup cooked dry beans, 1 egg or 2 tablespoons peanut butter count as 1 ounce lean meat

2-3 ounces cooked lean meat, poultry or fish

Vegetable Group

1 cup raw leafy vegetables

½ cup other vegetables, cooked or raw

¾ cup vegetable juice

Fruit Group

¾ cup fruit juice

½ cup chopped, cooked or canned fruit

1 medium apple, banana or orange

Bread, Cereal, Rice & Pasta Group

1 muffin, dinner roll or slice bread

1 ounce ready-to-eat cereal

½ cup cooked cereal, rice or pasta

2 Add juice, wine, sugar, salt, marjoram and pepper to skillet. Cover. Reduce heat to low. Let simmer for 12 to 15 minutes, or until meat near bone is no longer pink and juices run clear.

3 Remove chicken from skillet and place on serving platter. Cover to keep warm. Set aside. Using whisk, stir cornstarch mixture into skillet. Add grapes and peel. Cook for 1½ to 2½ minutes, or until sauce is thickened and translucent, stirring constantly. Spoon over chicken.

Nutrition Facts	Amount/serving	%DV*	Amount/serving	%DV*
Serving Size 1 breast half (136g)	Total Fat 5g	7%	Total Carbohydrate 9g	3%
	Saturated Fat 1g	5%	Dietary Fiber <1g	1%
Servings per Recipe 6	Cholesterol 55mg	18%	Sugars 8g	
Calories 164	Sodium 135mg	6%	Protein 21g	
Calories from Fat 41	Vitamin A 0% • Vitamin C 20% • Calcium 2% • Iron 4%			
	*Percent Daily Values (DV) are based on a 2000 calorie diet.			

Menu Planning Guide

One serving of this recipe provides:
1 Meat, Poultry & Fish
½ Fruit

Diet Exchanges:

3 lean meat • ½ fruit

Nutritional Information

Each recipe in this book is followed by a Nutrition Facts chart and diet exchanges. The Nutrition Facts chart is similar to those that appear on food product labels. The diet exchange system is used by people with diabetes and persons on a weight-control diet, to estimate the calories, protein, carbohydrate and fat content of a food or meal. Diet exchanges are based on exchange lists and are not the same as pyramid servings.

Nutrition Facts state serving size, servings per container and the amount of calories, calories from fat and other nutrients per serving. Percentage of Daily Value gives you an idea of what percentage of the day's nutrients comes from the recipe. The percentages of the Daily Value of fat, saturated fat, cholesterol, sodium, total carbohydrate and dietary fiber are based on a 2,000-calorie-per-day diet. (Daily values will vary from person to person depending on calorie needs.) The Dietary Guidelines recommend that no more than 30% of your calories come from fat. So, if you are eating 2,000 calories per day, your total fat intake should be less than 65 grams.

If alternate ingredients are given in the recipe's ingredient list, such as a choice between cholesterol-free egg product and egg, the nutritional analysis applies to the first ingredient listed. Optional ingredients are not included in the analysis. For pasta and rice, the nutritional information applies to the plain, boiled item without salt or fat added.

Recipe serving sizes are based on federal reference numbers for serving sizes.

The Pyramid in This Book

Each recipe in this book includes a Menu Planning Guide that shows the number of servings from each pyramid group that one serving of that recipe provides. A daily total of these "pyramid servings" shows how your diet compares to the USDA recommendations.

When the tip of the pyramid has a dot, the item may contain added fat or fat beyond the natural fat content of lean or low-fat items in the food groups. Refer to the Nutrition Facts chart to check the total amount of fat per serving. A tip with a dot may also indicate that the recipe contains added sugar. Refer to the recipe to determine the number of teaspoons of sugar you will eat.

The number of servings is rounded to the nearest half. If no figures appear next to or within the pyramid, it means that serving sizes are negligible.

If the tip of the pyramid has no dot, a serving contains less than 3 grams added fat or less than 1 teaspoon added sugar.

Beef Eye Round Steaks with Vegetables

*Serve with crisp salad with Creamy Horseradish Dressing (p 66)
and a dinner roll*

12 oz. new potatoes, sliced (2 cups), rinsed
   and drained

1 pkg. (10 oz.) frozen peas and carrots

1 cup water

1 tablespoon margarine

1 tablespoon all-purpose flour

½ teaspoon salt

½ teaspoon dried marjoram

¼ teaspoon pepper

¾ cup skim milk

4 beef eye round steaks (4 oz. each), ¾ inch
   thick

4 servings

1 Combine potatoes, peas, carrots and water in 3-quart saucepan. Cover. Cook over medium-high heat for 14 to 18 minutes, or until vegetables are tender, stirring occasionally. Drain. Return vegetables to saucepan. Cover to keep warm. Set aside.

2 Melt margarine in 1-quart saucepan over medium-low heat. Stir in flour, salt, marjoram and pepper. Gradually blend in milk. Cook for 7 to 12 minutes, or until mixture thickens and bubbles, stirring frequently. Add sauce to vegetable mixture. Toss to combine. Re-cover. Set aside.

3 Spray rack in broiler pan with nonstick vegetable cooking spray. Arrange steaks on rack. Place under broiler with surface of meat 3 to 5 inches from heat. Broil for 13 to 15 minutes, or until desired doneness, turning steaks over once. Serve steaks with vegetable mixture.

Grilling tip: Prepare as directed in steps 1 and 2. Spray cooking grid with nonstick vegetable cooking spray. Prepare grill for medium direct heat. Place steaks on cooking grid. Grill, covered, for 10 to 12 minutes, or until desired doneness, turning steaks over once.

Nutrition Facts	Amount/serving	%DV*	Amount/serving	%DV*
Serving Size 1 steak (294g)	Total Fat 8g	12%	Total Carbohydrate 27g	9%
Servings per Recipe 4	Saturated Fat 2g	12%	Dietary Fiber 4g	16%
Calories 303	Cholesterol 63mg	21%	Sugars 6g	
Calories from Fat 68	Sodium 431mg	18%	Protein 32g	

Vitamin A 110% • Vitamin C 30% • Calcium 8% • Iron 15%

*Percent Daily Values (DV) are based on a 2000 calorie diet.

Menu Planning Guide

One serving of this recipe provides:

1 Meat, Poultry & Fish
2 Vegetable

Diet Exchanges:

3 lean meat • 1½ starch • ½ vegetable

Brandy Pepper Steaks

Serve with Corn & Leek Pudding (p 84) and steamed new potatoes

4 beef eye round steaks (4 oz. each), ¾ inch
   thick
1 to 3 teaspoons coarsely ground pepper
½ cup ready-to-serve beef broth
2 teaspoons cornstarch
4 oz. fresh mushrooms, sliced (1½ cups)
¼ cup sliced green onions
1 tablespoon brandy
¼ teaspoon salt

4 servings

1 Sprinkle both sides of steaks evenly with pepper. Set aside. In 1-quart saucepan, combine broth and cornstarch. Stir until blended. Stir in mushrooms, onions, brandy and salt. Cook over medium heat for 3 to 4 minutes, or until mixture is thickened and translucent, stirring constantly. Cover to keep warm. Remove from heat. Set sauce aside.

2 Spray cooking grid with nonstick vegetable cooking spray. Prepare grill for medium direct heat. Place steaks on cooking grid. Grill, covered, for 10 to 12 minutes, or until desired doneness, turning steaks over once.

Nutrition Facts	Amount/serving	%DV*	Amount/serving	%DV*
	Total Fat 6g	9%	Total Carbohydrate 3g	1%
Serving Size 1 steak (158g)	Saturated Fat 2g	11%	Dietary Fiber 1g	3%
Servings per Recipe 4	Cholesterol 64mg	21%	Sugars 1g	
Calories 185 Calories from Fat 55	Sodium 286mg	12%	Protein 28g	

Vitamin A 0% • Vitamin C 4% • Calcium 2% • Iron 15%
*Percent Daily Values (DV) are based on a 2000 calorie diet.

Menu Planning Guide
One serving of this recipe provides:
  1 Meat, Poultry & Fish
½ Vegetable

Diet Exchanges:
1 lean meat • ½ vegetable

Broiled Fruited Pork Chops

Serve with Savory Wild Rice (p 97) and Double Artichoke Salad (p 69)

6 well-trimmed boneless pork loin chops
    (4 oz. each), 1/2 inch thick
1 can (8 oz.) pineapple slices in juice, drained
    (reserve 1/4 cup juice)
1 can (16 oz.) apricot halves in juice, drained
1/4 cup apricot preserves
2 teaspoons Dijon mustard
2 teaspoons cider vinegar

6 servings

1 Arrange pork chops on rack in broiler pan. Cut pineapple slices in half. Arrange pineapple and apricots evenly around chops. Set aside. In 1-quart saucepan, combine preserves, mustard and vinegar. Cook over low heat for 5 to 8 minutes, or until preserves are melted, stirring occasionally.

2 Brush chops with half of preserves mixture. Brush pineapple and apricots with half of reserved pineapple juice. Place chops under broiler with surface of meat 3 to 4 inches from heat. Broil for 10 to 12 minutes, or until desired doneness, turning chops over and basting chops with remaining preserves mixture and fruit with remaining juice once.

Microwave tip: In 2-cup measure, combine preserves, mustard and vinegar. Microwave at High for 2 to 3 minutes, or until preserves are melted, stirring once. Continue as directed.

Nutrition Facts	Amount/serving	%DV*	Amount/serving	%DV*
Serving Size 1 chop (207g)	Total Fat 7g	11%	Total Carbohydrate 22g	7%
Servings per Recipe 6	Saturated Fat 2g	12%	Dietary Fiber 2g	8%
Calories 252	Cholesterol 67mg	22%	Sugars 19g	
Calories from Fat 64	Sodium 77mg	3%	Protein 26g	

Vitamin A 35% • Vitamin C 25% • Calcium 4% • Iron 8%
*Percent Daily Values (DV) are based on a 2000 calorie diet.

Menu Planning Guide
One serving of this recipe provides:
1 Meat, Poultry & Fish
1 Fruit

Diet Exchanges:
3 lean meat • 1 1/2 fruit

Greek Burgers

Serve with Greek Salad (p 74) or Tabbouleh Salad (p 81)

¾ cup water

¼ cup uncooked bulgur (cracked wheat)

¼ cup plain nonfat or low-fat yogurt

½ teaspoon dried dill weed

1 cup finely chopped seeded cucumber

1 lb. lean ground beef, crumbled

½ to 1 teaspoon grated lemon peel

½ teaspoon dried oregano leaves

½ teaspoon salt

¼ teaspoon pepper

6 pita loaves (6-inch), warmed
   Leaf lettuce

12 slices tomato

6 servings

1 Bring water to boil in 1-quart saucepan over high heat. Remove from heat. Stir in bulgur. Cover. Let stand for 30 minutes, or until bulgur softens. Meanwhile, in small mixing bowl, combine yogurt, dill weed and cucumber. Cover with plastic wrap. Chill.

2 Combine beef, peel, oregano, salt and pepper in medium mixing bowl. Drain any excess water from bulgur. Add bulgur to beef mixture. Mix well. Form mixture into six ¾-inch-thick oval patties.

3 Place burgers on rack in broiler pan. Place under broiler with surface of meat 4 inches from heat. Broil burgers 8 to 10 minutes, or until desired doneness, turning burgers over once.

4 Fold each pita loaf in half. Place lettuce, 1 burger and 2 tomato slices in each pita. Spoon cucumber mixture evenly into each pita. Secure with wooden pick.

Grilling tip: Prepare as directed in steps 1, 2 and 4. Spray cooking grid with nonstick vegetable cooking spray. Prepare grill for medium direct heat. Place burgers on cooking grid. Grill, covered, for 8 to 10 minutes, or until desired doneness, turning burgers over once.

Nutrition Facts	Amount/serving	%DV*	Amount/serving	%DV*	Menu Planning Guide
Serving Size 1 burger (180g)	Total Fat 11g	17%	Total Carbohydrate 36g	12%	One serving of this recipe provides:
Servings per Recipe 6	Saturated Fat 4g	20%	Dietary Fiber 1g	6%	1 Meat, Poultry & Fish
Calories 337	Cholesterol 58mg	19%	Sugars 2g		2 Bread, Cereal, Rice & Pasta
Calories from Fat 97	Sodium 559mg	23%	Protein 22g		

Vitamin A 0% • Vitamin C 2% • Calcium 8% • Iron 20%
*Percent Daily Values (DV) are based on a 2000 calorie diet.

Diet Exchanges:
2 starch • 2 medium-fat meat

Greek Pork Tenderloin

Serve with Orzo Pasta (p 93), steamed broccoli spears and garlic toast

Stuffing:

1/3 cup chopped onion

1/2 teaspoon grated lemon peel

1 tablespoon fresh lemon juice, divided

1 clove garlic, minced

4 cups torn fresh spinach leaves

3 tablespoons crumbled feta cheese

2 teaspoons snipped fresh dill weed or
    1 teaspoon dried dill weed

1 - lb. well-trimmed pork tenderloin

1/4 teaspoon seasoned salt

1/4 teaspoon freshly ground pepper

4 servings

1 Spray 10-inch nonstick skillet with nonstick vegetable cooking spray. Add onion, peel, 1 teaspoon juice and the garlic. Cook over medium heat for 1 1/2 to 3 minutes, or until onion is tender-crisp, stirring frequently. Stir in spinach. Cook for additional 1 to 1 1/2 minutes, or until spinach is wilted, stirring constantly. Remove from heat. Stir in feta and dill weed. Set stuffing aside.

2 Cut tenderloin crosswise into 4 pieces. Make horizontal cut through center of pieces to within 1/2 inch of opposite sides; do not cut through. Open pieces like a book. Spoon and pack stuffing evenly down one side of each piece. Fold other sides over to enclose stuffing.

3 Tie pieces with string to secure. Brush evenly with remaining 2 teaspoons juice. Sprinkle evenly with salt and pepper. Arrange on rack in broiler pan. Place under broiler with surface of meat 5 to 7 inches from heat. Broil for 15 to 20 minutes, or until desired doneness, turning pieces over once. Let stand, tented with foil, for 5 minutes. (Internal temperature will rise 5°F during standing.)

Nutrition Facts	Amount/serving	%DV*	Amount/serving	%DV*
Serving Size 1 piece (177g)	Total Fat 7g	11%	Total Carbohydrate 5g	2%
Servings per Recipe 4	Saturated Fat 3g	15%	Dietary Fiber 2g	8%
Calories 198	Cholesterol 81mg	27%	Sugars 2g	
Calories from Fat 63	Sodium 327mg	14%	Protein 29g	

Vitamin A 90% • Vitamin C 15% • Calcium 15% • Iron 20%

*Percent Daily Values (DV) are based on a 2000 calorie diet.

Menu Planning Guide
One serving of this recipe provides:
1 Meat, Poultry & Fish
1 Vegetable

Diet Exchanges:
3 1/2 lean meat • 1 vegetable

Herbed Flank Steak Sandwiches

Serve with Lemon Broccoli & Cauliflower Salad (p 77) or Rosemary New Potatoes & Beans (p 94)

1   tablespoon vegetable oil

⅓   cup chopped onion

1   clove garlic, minced

⅓   cup red wine vinegar

2   tablespoons packed brown sugar

1   tablespoon snipped fresh parsley

1   tablespoon snipped fresh oregano leaves

1   tablespoon fresh thyme leaves

1-lb. well-trimmed beef flank steak

4   kaiser rolls, split

   Sweet hot mustard

8   slices tomato

   Lettuce leaves

4 servings

1 Place oil in 1-quart saucepan. Heat over medium-low heat. Add onion and garlic. Cook for 3 to 4 minutes, or until onion is tender, stirring occasionally. Add vinegar, sugar, parsley, oregano and thyme. Mix well. Set aside to cool.

2 Score steak with 6 diagonal slashes, about ⅛ inch deep. Place steak in large plastic food-storage bag. Add marinade. Secure bag. Turn to coat. Chill 6 hours or overnight, turning bag occasionally.

3 Spray cooking grid with nonstick vegetable cooking spray. Prepare grill for medium direct heat. Drain and discard marinade from meat. Place steak on cooking grid. Grill, covered, for 12 to 14 minutes, or until desired doneness, turning steak over once.

4 Carve steak across grain into thin slices. Spread cut sides of each roll with mustard. Top evenly with steak, tomato and lettuce.

Microwave tip: In 2-cup measure, combine oil, onion and garlic. Cover with plastic wrap. Microwave at High for 2 to 3 minutes, or until onion is tender, stirring once. Continue as directed.

Nutrition Facts	Amount/serving	%DV*	Amount/serving	%DV*
Serving Size 1 sandwich (188g)	Total Fat 13g	20%	Total Carbohydrate 32g	11%
Servings per Recipe 4	Saturated Fat 4g	19%	Dietary Fiber 1g	4%
Calories 360	Cholesterol 57mg	19%	Sugars 3g	
Calories from Fat 110	Sodium 413mg	17%	Protein 29g	

Vitamin A 2% • Vitamin C 15% • Calcium 2% • Iron 30%

*Percent Daily Values (DV) are based on a 2000 calorie diet.

Menu Planning Guide

One serving of this recipe provides:

1 Meat, Poultry & Fish

2 Bread, Cereal, Rice & Pasta

Diet Exchanges:

3 lean meat • 2 starch

Honey-Mustard Chops & Carrots

Serve with Spicy Apple Slaw (p 78) and Tri-bean Bake (p 106)

1/4 cup plus 1 tablespoon honey

2 tablespoons packed brown sugar

2 to 3 tablespoons Dijon mustard

1 pkg. (14 oz.) frozen whole baby carrots

1/4 cup water

4 well-trimmed boneless pork loin chops
   (4 oz. each), 3/4 inch thick

4 servings

1 Combine honey, sugar and mustard in 1-quart saucepan. Cook over medium heat for 2 to 3 minutes, or until sugar is dissolved, stirring frequently. Set glaze aside.

2 Combine carrots and water in 2-quart saucepan. Cover. Cook over high heat for 8 to 9 minutes, or until hot, stirring occasionally. Drain. Add 3 tablespoons glaze to carrots. Toss to coat. Cover. Set aside.

3 Prepare grill for medium direct heat. Spray cooking grid with nonstick vegetable cooking spray. Place chops on cooking grid. Grill, covered, for 9 to 13 minutes, or until desired doneness, turning and basting with remaining glaze 3 or 4 times. Arrange pork chops on serving platter. Serve with carrots.

Microwave tip: In 2-cup measure, combine honey, sugar and mustard. Microwave at High for 2 to 2½ minutes, or until sugar is dissolved, stirring once. Continue as directed.

Nutrition Facts	Amount/serving	%DV*	Amount/serving	%DV*
Serving Size 1 chop with ½ cup carrots (200g)	Total Fat 8g	12%	Total Carbohydrate 35g	12%
	Saturated Fat 3g	14%	Dietary Fiber 3g	12%
Servings per Recipe 4	Cholesterol 64mg	21%	Sugars 28g	
Calories 309 Calories from Fat 73	Sodium 320mg	13%	Protein 24g	
	Vitamin A 390% • Vitamin C 4% • Calcium 4% • Iron 10%			
	*Percent Daily Values (DV) are based on a 2000 calorie diet.			

Menu Planning Guide

One serving of this recipe provides:

1 Meat, Poultry & Fish
1 Vegetable

Diet Exchanges:

2½ lean meat • 2 starch • 1 vegetable

Rosemary Butterflied Leg of Lamb

Serve with Tabbouleh Salad (p 81) or roasted new potatoes and Colorful Marinated Vegetables (p 83)

Marinade:

1½ cups port wine

¾ cup red wine vinegar

8 cloves garlic, minced

2 tablespoons snipped fresh rosemary leaves

4 -lb. well-trimmed boneless butterflied
   lamb leg*

16 servings

Order butterflied lamb leg from meat cutter.

1 Combine marinade ingredients in 4-cup measure. Reserve ½ cup marinade. Cover with plastic wrap. Chill. Place lamb in large plastic food-storage bag. Add remaining marinade. Secure bag. Turn to coat. Chill 2 to 3 hours, turning bag occasionally.

2 Spray cooking grid with nonstick vegetable cooking spray. Prepare grill for medium direct heat. Drain and discard marinade from lamb. Place lamb cut-side-up on grid. Grill, covered, for 25 to 30 minutes (rare, 140°F), or until desired doneness, basting occasionally with reserved marinade. Let stand, tented with foil, for 10 minutes before carving.

Nutrition Facts	Amount/serving	%DV*	Amount/serving	%DV*
Serving Size 3 oz. (88g)	Total Fat 6g	9%	Total Carbohydrate 0g	0%
Servings per Recipe 16	Saturated Fat 2g	10%	Dietary Fiber 0g	0%
Calories 154	Cholesterol 74mg	25%	Sugars 0g	
Calories from Fat 51	Sodium 58mg	2%	Protein 24g	

Vitamin A 0% • Vitamin C 0% • Calcium 0% • Iron 10%
*Percent Daily Values (DV) are based on a 2000 calorie diet.

Menu Planning Guide

One serving of this recipe provides:

1 Meat, Poultry & Fish

Diet Exchanges:

3 lean meat

Rum-spiced Pork Chops

Serve with Black Bean & Mango Salad (p 63) and oven-fried potatoes

2   teaspoons olive oil

1   large onion, finely chopped (1⅓ cups)

¼   cup finely chopped green onions

2   habañero, serrano or other hot chili peppers,
    seeded and finely chopped

4   cloves garlic, minced

1   bay leaf

½   teaspoon dried thyme leaves

½   teaspoon ground cinnamon

⅛   teaspoon ground nutmeg

⅛   teaspoon ground cloves

¼   cup dark rum

2   tablespoons fresh lime juice

¼   teaspoon salt

4   well-trimmed bone-in pork loin chops
    (6 oz. each), ¾ to 1 inch thick

4 servings

1 Heat oil in 10-inch nonstick skillet over medium heat. Add onions, peppers, garlic, bay leaf, thyme, cinnamon, nutmeg and cloves. Cook for 10 to 12 minutes, or until mixture is deep golden brown, stirring frequently.

2 Increase heat to medium-high. Stir in rum, juice and salt. Cook for 1½ to 2½ minutes, or until most of liquid boils off. Remove from heat. Remove and discard bay leaf. Cool marinade completely.

3 Place pork chops in shallow dish. Spread marinade evenly over chops, turning chops over once to coat. Cover with plastic wrap. Refrigerate 4 hours or overnight.

4 Prepare grill for medium-high direct heat. Spray cooking grid with nonstick vegetable cooking spray. Place chops on cooking grid. (Do not remove marinade from meat.) Grill chops, covered, for 12 to 15 minutes, or just until meat is no longer pink, turning chops over once.

Nutrition Facts	Amount/serving	%DV*	Amount/serving	%DV*
Serving Size 1 chop (195g)	Total Fat 10g	16%	Total Carbohydrate 10g	3%
Servings per Recipe 4	Saturated Fat 3g	15%	Dietary Fiber 2g	6%
Calories 266	Cholesterol 80mg	27%	Sugars 5g	
Calories from Fat 93	Sodium 203mg	8%	Protein 33g	

Vitamin A 30% • Vitamin C 70% • Calcium 6% • Iron 10%
*Percent Daily Values (DV) are based on a 2000 calorie diet.

Menu Planning Guide

One serving of this recipe provides:
1   Meat, Poultry & Fish
1   Vegetable

Diet Exchanges:

4 lean meat • 1 vegetable

Teriyaki Steak & Vegetable Kabobs

Serve with Tangy Lime Risotto (p 101) or a baked potato

1/3 cup reduced-sodium teriyaki sauce
 2 tablespoons packed brown sugar
 2 cloves garlic, minced
 1 teaspoon freshly grated ginger
1/4 teaspoon freshly ground pepper
 1-lb. well-trimmed beef top round steak,
    1 inch thick
 8 pearl onions, peeled
 4 small new potatoes, halved (about 6 oz.)
1/2 cup water
16 cherry tomatoes
 1 small green pepper, cut into 8 chunks
    (1-inch chunks)

4 servings

1 Soak eight 6-inch wooden skewers in water for 1/2 hour. In 1-quart saucepan, combine teriyaki sauce, sugar, garlic, ginger and pepper. Cook over medium-low heat for 1 to 2 minutes, or until sugar is dissolved, stirring constantly. Score top of steak in diamond pattern, cutting 1/8 inch deep. Place steak in shallow dish. Pour 1/4 cup teriyaki mixture over steak. Turn to coat. Set aside.

2 Combine onions, potatoes and water in 2-quart saucepan. Bring water to boil over medium-high heat. Cover. Reduce heat to low. Simmer for 13 to 15 minutes, or until potatoes are tender. Drain. Thread 1 tomato, 1 potato half, 1 pepper chunk, 1 onion and 1 tomato on each skewer. Place steak scored-side-up on rack in broiler pan. Arrange kabobs evenly around steak.

3 Brush steak and kabobs with half of reserved teriyaki mixture. Place under broiler, with surface of meat 3 to 4 inches from heat. Broil for 14 to 16 minutes, or until meat is desired doneness, turning kabobs over and brushing steak and kabobs once with remaining reserved teriyaki mixture.

Nutrition Facts	Amount/serving	%DV*	Amount/serving	%DV*
Serving Size 1/4 recipe (253g)	Total Fat 4g	7%	Total Carbohydrate 23g	8%
	Saturated Fat 1g	7%	Dietary Fiber 3g	11%
Servings per Recipe 4	Cholesterol 70mg	23%	Sugars 9g	
Calories 244 Calories from Fat 40	Sodium 261mg	11%	Protein 28g	

Vitamin A 6% • Vitamin C 60% • Calcium 2% • Iron 20%
*Percent Daily Values (DV) are based on a 2000 calorie diet.

Menu Planning Guide
One serving of this recipe provides:
1 Meat, Poultry & Fish
1 Vegetable

Diet Exchanges:
3 lean meat • 1 starch

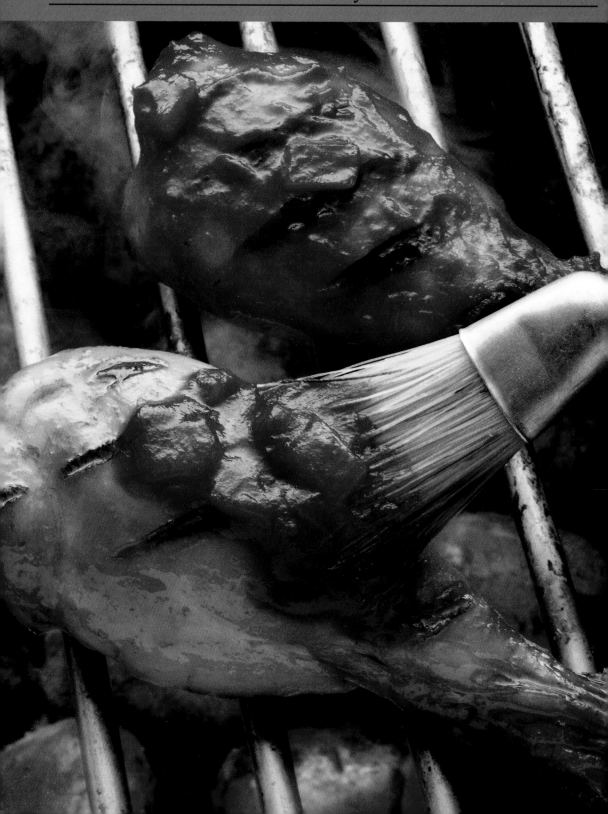

BBQ Chicken

Serve with Three-bean Medley (p 102)
and Seasoned Potato Wedges (p 98)

BBQ Sauce:

1/4 cup finely chopped onion

1 teaspoon vegetable oil

1 can (8 oz.) tomato sauce

3 tablespoons packed brown sugar

2 tablespoons tomato paste

2 tablespoons red wine vinegar

2 teaspoons Worcestershire sauce

2 cloves garlic, minced

1 teaspoon dry mustard

1/8 teaspoon cayenne

3 to 5 drops red pepper sauce

3-lb. whole broiler-fryer chicken, cut into
    8 pieces, skin removed

8 servings

1 Combine onion and oil in 1-quart saucepan. Cook over medium heat for 3 to 5 minutes, or until onion is tender, stirring frequently. Stir in remaining sauce ingredients. Bring to boil. Reduce heat to low. Simmer for 20 to 25 minutes, or until sauce is desired thickness. Reserve 1/2 cup sauce. Set remaining sauce aside.

2 Prepare grill for medium direct heat. Spray cooking grid with nonstick vegetable cooking spray. Grill chicken, covered, for 20 to 25 minutes, or until meat near bone is no longer pink and juices run clear, turning chicken over occasionally and basting with remaining sauce 2 or 3 times during last 5 to 8 minutes of grilling. Serve chicken with reserved sauce.

Nutrition Facts	Amount/serving	%DV*	Amount/serving	%DV*
Serving Size 1 piece chicken (109g)	Total Fat 5g	8%	Total Carbohydrate 7g	2%
	Saturated Fat 1g	7%	Dietary Fiber 1g	4%
Servings per Recipe 8	Cholesterol 55mg	18%	Sugars 5g	
	Sodium 270mg	11%	Protein 18g	
Calories 152 Calories from Fat 48	Vitamin A 8% • Vitamin C 10% • Calcium 2% • Iron 8%			
	*Percent Daily Values (DV) are based on a 2000 calorie diet.			

Menu Planning Guide

One serving of this recipe provides:

1 Meat, Poultry & Fish

Diet Exchanges:

2 1/2 lean meat • 1/2 vegetable

Cajun Chicken Divan

*Serve with a spinach salad with tomatoes
or Dixie Vegetable Dish (p 86) and a dinner roll*

2 tablespoons margarine
3 tablespoons all-purpose flour, divided
1 clove garlic, minced
1½ cups skim milk
½ teaspoon cayenne, divided
¼ teaspoon salt
½ teaspoon dried oregano leaves
⅛ teaspoon onion powder
2 boneless whole chicken breasts (8 to 10 oz.
   each), split in half, skin removed
½ cup water
3 cups broccoli flowerets
2 cups hot cooked fettucini

4 servings

1 Melt margarine in 1-quart saucepan over medium-low heat. Stir in 2 tablespoons flour. Cook for 3 to 8 minutes, or until mixture is light golden brown, stirring frequently. Stir in remaining 1 tablespoon flour and the garlic. Cook for 1 minute, stirring constantly. Gradually whisk in milk. Cook for 5 to 12 minutes, or until sauce thickens and bubbles, stirring constantly. Remove from heat. Stir in ¼ teaspoon cayenne and the salt. Cover to keep warm. Set sauce aside.

2 Prepare grill for medium direct heat. Spray cooking grid with nonstick vegetable cooking spray. In small bowl, combine remaining ¼ teaspoon cayenne, the oregano and onion powder. Rub mixture evenly on both sides of chicken breasts. Place chicken on prepared grid. Grill, covered, for 10 to 12 minutes, or until meat is no longer pink and juices run clear, turning chicken over once.

3 Slice breasts crosswise into 1-inch strips. Cover to keep warm. Set aside. In 2-quart saucepan, bring water to boil over medium-high heat. Add broccoli. Cover. Cook for 2 to 3 minutes, or just until color brightens. Drain well. Stir broccoli into sauce. To serve, spoon sauce over fettucini. Top with chicken strips.

Nutrition Facts	Amount/serving	%DV*	Amount/serving	%DV*
Serving Size approximately 1 cup (367g)	Total Fat 10g	15%	Total Carbohydrate 35g	12%
	Saturated Fat 2g	11%	Dietary Fiber 5g	19%
Servings per Recipe 4	Cholesterol 64mg	21%	Sugars 8g	
Calories 360 Calories from Fat 86	Sodium 383mg	14%	Protein 34g	

Vitamin A 45% • Vitamin C 150% • Calcium 20% • Iron 20%
*Percent Daily Values (DV) are based on a 2000 calorie diet.

Menu Planning Guide
One serving of this recipe provides:
½ Milk, Yogurt & Cheese
1 Meat, Poultry & Fish
1½ Vegetable
1 Bread, Cereal, Rice & Pasta

Diet Exchanges:
2½ lean meat • 1 skim milk • 1½ starch
• 1½ vegetable • 1 fat

Chicken Kabobs with Poppy Seed Baste

Serve with Confetti Cabbage Slaw (p 64) and a baked potato

3/4 cup honey

3/4 cup white vinegar

1 1/2 tablespoons Dijon mustard

2 boneless whole chicken breasts
   (8 to 10 oz. each), split in half,
   skin removed, cut into 3/4-inch strips

2 teaspoons cornstarch mixed
   with 2 teaspoons water

1 to 2 teaspoons poppy seed

1/2 green pepper, cut into 1-inch chunks

1/2 red pepper, cut into 1-inch chunks

1 small yellow squash, cut in half lengthwise,
   then crosswise into 1/2-inch slices

2 small onions, cut into quarters

8 whole fresh mushrooms

4 servings

1 Combine honey, vinegar and mustard in 2-cup measure. Reserve 3/4 cup honey mixture. Set aside. In small mixing bowl, combine remaining honey mixture and chicken. Cover with plastic wrap. Chill 30 minutes, stirring occasionally. Meanwhile, soak eight 10-inch wooden skewers in water for 30 minutes. Set aside.

2 Combine reserved honey mixture and cornstarch mixture in 1-quart saucepan. Cook over medium heat for 4 to 8 minutes, or until thickened and translucent, stirring frequently. Remove from heat. Stir in poppy seed. Set poppy seed mixture aside.

3 Prepare grill for medium direct heat. Spray cooking grid with nonstick vegetable cooking spray. Drain and discard marinade from chicken. On skewers, evenly thread chicken accordion-style and skewer 3 or more pieces of remaining ingredients.

4 Place kabobs on cooking grid. Grill, covered, for 10 to 12 minutes, or until meat is firm and no longer pink and vegetables are desired doneness, turning kabobs over and basting with poppy seed mixture 2 or 3 times.

Nutrition Facts	Amount/serving	%DV*	Amount/serving	%DV*	Menu Planning Guide
Serving Size 2 kabobs (288g)	Total Fat 4g	5%	Total Carbohydrate 39g	13%	One serving of this recipe provides:
Servings per Recipe 4	Saturated Fat <1g	4%	Dietary Fiber 2g	8%	1 Meat, Poultry & Fish 1 Vegetable
Calories 276	Cholesterol 60mg	20%	Sugars 32g		
Calories from Fat 32	Sodium 131mg	5%	Protein 25g		
	Vitamin A 10% • Vitamin C 50% • Calcium 6% • Iron 10%				**Diet Exchanges:**
	*Percent Daily Values (DV) are based on a 2000 calorie diet.				2 1/2 lean meat • 2 starch • 1 vegetable

Herbed Cornish Game Hens

Serve with Colorful Marinated Vegetables (p 83) and Orzo Pasta (p 93)

1 tablespoon snipped fresh rosemary leaves

2 teaspoons dried basil leaves

2 Cornish game hens (20 to 24 oz. each), split
   in half lengthwise

⅔ cup ready-to-serve chicken broth

⅓ cup fresh orange juice

⅔ cup uncooked couscous

½ teaspoon grated orange peel

1 tablespoon snipped fresh parsley

4 servings

1 Combine rosemary and basil in small bowl. Reserve 1 teaspoon herb mixture. Lift skin on 1 hen half and rub 1 teaspoon remaining herb mixture evenly between meat and skin. Pull skin over herb mixture. Repeat with remaining hen halves and 3 teaspoons herb mixture.

2 Spray rack in broiler pan with nonstick vegetable cooking spray. Arrange hen halves skin-side-up on rack. Spray hens with nonstick vegetable cooking spray. Sprinkle reserved herb mixture evenly over hens.

3 Place hens under broiler, with surface of meat 3 to 5 inches from heat. Broil for 30 to 35 minutes, or until meat near bone is no longer pink and juices run clear, turning hens over once.

4 Meanwhile, combine broth and juice in 1-quart saucepan. Bring to boil over medium-high heat. Stir in couscous and peel. Remove from heat. Cover. Let stand for 5 minutes. Stir in parsley. Serve hen halves over couscous. Before eating, remove and discard skin from hens.

Nutrition Facts	Amount/serving	%DV*	Amount/serving	%DV*
Serving Size ½ hen with couscous (292g)	Total Fat 10g	15%	Total Carbohydrate 27g	9%
	Saturated Fat 3g	13%	Dietary Fiber 2g	8%
Servings per Recipe 4	Cholesterol 110mg	37%	Sugars 3g	
Calories 373 Calories from Fat 88	Sodium 530mg	22%	Protein 41g	

Vitamin A 6% • Vitamin C 20% • Calcium 6% • Iron 15%

*Percent Daily Values (DV) are based on a 2000 calorie diet.

Menu Planning Guide

One serving of this recipe provides:

2 Meat, Poultry & Fish
1 Bread, Cereal, Rice & Pasta

Diet Exchanges:

4½ lean meat • 1½ starch

Tequila Turkey

Serve with Mexicali Corn on the Cob (p 91) and Tangy Lime Risotto (p 101) or Seasoned Potato Wedges (p 98)

Relish:

- 1 medium tomato, seeded and chopped (1 cup)
- 1/2 cup finely chopped yellow pepper
- 2 tablespoons snipped fresh cilantro leaves or Italian parsley
- 2 tablespoons red wine vinegar
- 1 jalapeño pepper, seeded and finely chopped
- 2 turkey tenderloins (8 to 10 oz. each)

Marinade:

- 1/3 cup fresh lime juice
- 1/4 cup tequila
- 2 teaspoons olive oil
- 1/4 teaspoon salt
- 1/4 teaspoon freshly ground pepper

4 servings

1 Combine relish ingredients in small mixing bowl. Cover with plastic wrap. Chill.

2 Place tenderloins in shallow dish. In 2-cup measure, combine marinade ingredients. Pour over tenderloins, turning tenderloins to coat. Cover with plastic wrap. Chill at least 2 hours, turning tenderloins over occasionally.

3 Drain and discard marinade from tenderloins. Prepare grill for medium-high direct heat. Spray cooking grid with non-stick vegetable cooking spray. Grill tenderloins for 20 to 25 minutes, or until meat is no longer pink and juices run clear. Thinly slice tenderloins across the grain. Serve with relish.

Nutrition Facts	Amount/serving	%DV*	Amount/serving	%DV*
Serving Size 1/2 tenderloin (141g)	Total Fat 1g	2%	Total Carbohydrate 3g	1%
Servings per Recipe 4	Saturated Fat 0g	0%	Dietary Fiber 1g	4%
Calories 130	Cholesterol 71mg	23%	Sugars 1g	
Calories from Fat 13	Sodium 84mg	4%	Protein 26g	

Vitamin A 6% • Vitamin C 60% • Calcium 2% • Iron 8%
*Percent Daily Values (DV) are based on a 2000 calorie diet.

Menu Planning Guide
One serving of this recipe provides:
1 Meat, Poultry & Fish

Diet Exchanges:
3 lean meat

Broiled Pesto Halibut Steaks

Serve with Rosemary New Potatoes & Beans (p 94)
or Savory Wild Rice (p 97) and a mixed green salad

½ cup tightly packed fresh basil leaves
3 tablespoons fat-free Italian dressing
1 clove garlic, minced
⅛ to ¼ teaspoon freshly ground pepper
4 halibut steaks (4 oz. each), ¾ inch thick

4 servings

1 Combine basil, dressing, garlic and pepper in food processor or blender. Process until basil is finely chopped. Set pesto aside. Spray rack in broiler pan with non-stick vegetable cooking spray. Arrange steaks on rack.

2 Brush steaks with half of pesto. Place under broiler with surface of fish 6 inches from heat. Broil for 5 minutes. Turn steaks over. Brush with remaining pesto. Broil for 6 to 7 minutes, or until fish is firm and opaque and just begins to flake.

Nutrition Facts	Amount/serving	%DV*	Amount/serving	%DV*
Serving Size 1 steak (109g)	Total Fat 3g	4%	Total Carbohydrate 1g	0%
Servings per Recipe 4	Saturated Fat <1g	2%	Dietary Fiber <1g	1%
Calories 132	Cholesterol 36mg	12%	Sugars 1g	
Calories from Fat 24	Sodium 219mg	9%	Protein 24g	

Vitamin A 10% • Vitamin C 4% • Calcium 6% • Iron 8%
*Percent Daily Values (DV) are based on a 2000 calorie diet.

Menu Planning Guide
One serving of this recipe provides:
1 Meat, Poultry & Fish

Diet Exchanges:
3 lean meat

Fresh Tuna Burgers

Serve with Fennel & Orange Salad (p 71)
or Grilled Yellow Squash & Zucchini Fans (p 108)

Sauce:

¼ *cup plain nonfat or low-fat yogurt*

1 *tablespoon diagonally sliced green onion*

½ *teaspoon packed brown sugar*

¼ *teaspoon grated fresh gingerroot*

4 *yellowfin tuna fillets (4 oz. each), ¾ inch thick*

Marinade:

¼ *cup rice wine vinegar*

2 *tablespoons peanut oil*

1 *tablespoon lemon juice*

1 *tablespoon water*

1 *tablespoon sugar*

2 *teaspoons grated fresh gingerroot*

1 *teaspoon low-sodium teriyaki sauce*

⅛ *teaspoon white pepper*

½ *yellow pepper, cut lengthwise into 8 strips*

½ *red pepper, cut lengthwise into 8 strips*

4 *whole-grain buns (2 oz. each), split*

4 servings

1 Combine sauce ingredients in small bowl. Cover with plastic wrap. Chill. Place fillets in shallow dish. In 1-cup measure, combine marinade ingredients. Pour over fillets, turning over once to coat. Cover dish with plastic wrap. Chill 2 hours, turning fillets over once.

2 Prepare grill for medium direct heat. Spray cooking grid with nonstick vegetable cooking spray. Drain and discard marinade from fillets. Place fillets on grid. Arrange pepper strips around fillets on grid. Grill, covered, for 15 to 18 minutes, or until fish is firm and just begins to flake, turning fillets and pepper strips over once.

3 Spread 1 tablespoon sauce on bottom half of each bun. Top evenly with fillets and pepper strips. Place top half of bun over pepper strips.

Nutrition Facts	Amount/serving	%DV*	Amount/serving	%DV*
Serving Size 1 burger (178g)	Total Fat 4g	7%	Total Carbohydrate 26g	9%
Servings per Recipe 4	Saturated Fat 1g	5%	Dietary Fiber 1g	5%
Calories 282	Cholesterol 55mg	18%	Sugars 6g	
Calories from Fat 40	Sodium 309mg	13%	Protein 33g	
	Vitamin A 15% • Vitamin C 60% • Calcium 10% • Iron 15%			
	*Percent Daily Values (DV) are based on a 2000 calorie diet.			

Menu Planning Guide

One serving of this recipe provides:
1 Meat, Poultry & Fish
2 Bread, Cereal, Rice & Pasta

Diet Exchanges:

3 lean meat • 2 starch

Halibut Vera Cruz

*Serve with Black Bean & Mango Salad (p 63)
and Tangy Lime Rissoto (p 101)*

Chutney:

- 2 ripe mangos, peeled and cut into ¼-inch cubes (2 cups)
- 1 cup packed brown sugar
- ½ cup thinly sliced green onions
- ¼ cup cider vinegar
- ¼ cup finely chopped green pepper
- 2 tablespoons grated fresh gingerroot
- 1 red chili pepper, seeded and finely chopped
- ¼ teaspoon ground cloves
- ⅛ teaspoon pepper

- 8 fresh halibut steaks (4 oz. each), ¾ inch thick
- ¼ teaspoon salt
- ¼ teaspoon pepper

8 servings

Tip: Chutney can be served chilled. Use as a condiment for meats, poultry, baked potatoes and curried dishes.

1 Combine chutney ingredients in 2-quart saucepan. Cook over medium-low heat for 25 to 35 minutes, or until mango is soft and chutney is thickened, stirring occasionally. Remove from heat. Cool slightly.

2 Meanwhile, prepare grill for medium direct heat. Spray cooking grid with nonstick vegetable cooking spray. Sprinkle steaks evenly with salt and pepper. Grill, covered, for 6 to 8 minutes, or until fish is firm and opaque and just begins to flake, turning over once. Serve steaks with chutney.

Nutrition Facts	Amount/serving	%DV*	Amount/serving	%DV*
Serving Size 1 steak with chutney (183g)	Total Fat 3g	4%	Total Carbohydrate 36g	12%
	Saturated Fat 0g	0%	Dietary Fiber 2g	6%
Servings per Recipe 8	Cholesterol 36mg	12%	Sugars 34g	
Calories 262	Sodium 141mg	6%	Protein 24g	
Calories from Fat 25	Vitamin A 50% • Vitamin C 50% • Calcium 8% • Iron 10%			
	*Percent Daily Values (DV) are based on a 2000 calorie diet.			

Menu Planning Guide

One serving of this recipe provides:

1 Meat, Poultry & Fish
½ Fruit

Diet Exchanges:

3 lean meat • 2 starch • ½ fruit

Orange-sauced Roughy

*Serve with Tangy Lime Risotto (p 101) and steamed
pea pods and carrots*

½ cup fresh orange juice
⅓ cup ready-to-serve chicken broth
    or dry white wine
 2 teaspoons cornstarch
 1 teaspoon sugar
¼ teaspoon dried thyme leaves
 1 lb. orange roughy fillets, about ½ inch
    thick, cut into serving-size pieces
 1 teaspoon vegetable oil

4 servings

1 Combine juice, broth, cornstarch, sugar
and thyme in 1-quart saucepan. Cook
over medium heat for 3 to 5 minutes, or
until sauce is thickened and translucent, stirring constantly. Remove from heat. Set aside.

2 Heat broiler. Spray large baking sheet
with nonstick vegetable cooking spray.
Arrange fillets on sheet. Brush fillets evenly
with oil.

3 Place under broiler with surface of fillets
5 inches from heat. Broil for 9 to 13 minutes, or until fish is firm and opaque and
just begins to flake. Arrange fish on serving
platter. Top with sauce.

Microwave tip: In 2-cup measure, combine juice, broth,
cornstarch, sugar and thyme. Microwave at High for 2½
to 4½ minutes, or until sauce is thickened and translucent, stirring once or twice. Continue as directed.

Nutrition Facts	Amount/serving	%DV*	Amount/serving	%DV*
Serving Size 1 fillet (143g)	Total Fat 2g	3%	Total Carbohydrate 6g	2%
	Saturated Fat <1g	1%	Dietary Fiber <1g	0%
Servings per Recipe 4	Cholesterol 23mg	8%	Sugars 4g	
Calories 114	Sodium 136mg	6%	Protein 17g	
Calories from Fat 19	Vitamin A 2% • Vitamin C 20% • Calcium 4% • Iron 2%			
	*Percent Daily Values (DV) are based on a 2000 calorie diet.			

Menu Planning Guide

One serving of this recipe provides:
1 Meat, Poultry & Fish

Diet Exchanges:

3 lean meat

Salmon Croquettes

Serve with Garlic Green Beans (p 89)
and Seasoned Potato Wedges (p 98)

1/4 cup finely chopped onion

2 tablespoons finely chopped celery

1/2 teaspoon vegetable oil

1 can (6½ oz.) skinless boneless salmon in
    water, rinsed and drained

1 cup cold mashed potatoes

1/4 cup sliced green onions

2 tablespoons snipped fresh parsley

1 egg white

1 tablespoon fresh lemon juice

3/4 teaspoon paprika, divided

1/2 teaspoon dry mustard

1/2 teaspoon garlic powder

1/4 teaspoon cayenne

1/4 cup unseasoned dry bread crumbs

Sauce:

1/2 cup nonfat or low-fat sour cream

2 teaspoons prepared mustard

1/2 teaspoon sugar

1/4 teaspoon dried dill weed

4 servings

1 Spray baking sheet with nonstick vegetable cooking spray. Set aside. In 8-inch nonstick skillet, combine chopped onion, celery and oil. Cook over medium heat for 4½ to 6½ minutes, or until vegetables are tender, stirring frequently.

2 Combine onion mixture, salmon, potatoes, green onions, parsley, egg white, juice, ¼ teaspoon paprika, the dry mustard, garlic powder and cayenne in medium mixing bowl. Form mixture into four 3-inch patties. In shallow dish, combine bread crumbs and remaining ½ teaspoon paprika. Dredge patties in bread crumb mixture to coat.

3 Arrange patties on prepared baking sheet. Place under broiler with surface of patties 4 to 5 inches from heat. Broil for 10 to 13 minutes, or until golden brown, turning patties over after half the time. Cover croquettes to keep warm. Set aside.

4 Combine sauce ingredients in 1-quart saucepan. Cook over low heat for 1½ to 3 minutes, or until sauce is hot, stirring constantly. Serve sauce over croquettes.

Microwave tip: In 1-cup measure, combine sauce ingredients. Microwave at Medium Low for 2½ to 5 minutes, or until sauce is hot, stirring once. Serve sauce over croquettes.

Nutrition Facts	Amount/serving	%DV*	Amount/serving	%DV*
Serving Size 1 croquette (157g)	Total Fat 4g	6%	Total Carbohydrate 19g	6%
Servings per Recipe 4	Saturated Fat 1g	4%	Dietary Fiber 2g	7%
Calories 161	Cholesterol 22mg	7%	Sugars 3g	
Calories from Fat 33	Sodium 158mg	7%	Protein 13g	
	Vitamin A 8% • Vitamin C 20% • Calcium 10% • Iron 8%			
	*Percent Daily Values (DV) are based on a 2000 calorie diet.			

Menu Planning Guide

One serving of this recipe provides:
1/2 Meat, Poultry & Fish
1/2 Vegetable

Diet Exchanges:

1½ lean meat • 1 starch

Swordfish with Creole Relish

Serve with Dixie Vegetable Dish (p 86) and a baked potato

1/2 cup chopped seeded tomato

1/4 cup chopped red pepper

1/4 cup finely chopped celery

1/4 cup finely chopped onion

1 tablespoon plus 1 teaspoon lemon juice, divided

1 clove garlic, minced

1 teaspoon vegetable oil

1/2 teaspoon dried oregano leaves

1/4 teaspoon dried basil leaves

1/4 teaspoon dried thyme leaves

1/4 teaspoon sugar

1/8 teaspoon salt

3 to 5 drops red pepper sauce

2 swordfish or halibut steaks (8 oz. each), about 1 inch thick

4 servings

1 Combine tomato and red pepper in blender. Process until nearly smooth. Set aside. Spray 7-inch nonstick skillet with non-stick vegetable cooking spray. Place celery, onion, 1 teaspoon juice, the garlic and oil in skillet. Cook over medium heat for 5 to 7 minutes, or until vegetables are tender-crisp, stirring frequently. Stir in tomato mixture and remaining ingredients, except swordfish and remaining juice. Cook for 3 to 4 minutes, or until liquid is reduced and relish thickens, stirring frequently. Remove from heat. Cover to keep warm. Set relish aside.

2 Cut each steak in half crosswise to yield 4 serving-size pieces. Spray broiler pan with nonstick vegetable cooking spray. Arrange steaks on rack in broiler pan. Sprinkle steaks evenly with remaining 1 tablespoon juice.

3 Place under broiler with surface of steaks 4 to 6 inches from heat. Broil for 4 to 6 minutes, or until fish is firm and opaque and just begins to flake. Serve each steak with about 3 tablespoons relish.

Grilling tip: Prepare as directed in steps 1 and 2. Spray cooking grid with nonstick vegetable cooking spray. Prepare grill for medium direct heat. Place steaks on grid. Grill, covered, for 6 to 8 minutes, or until fish is firm and opaque and just begins to flake.

Nutrition Facts	Amount/serving	%DV*	Amount/serving	%DV*
	Total Fat 6g	9%	Total Carbohydrate 4g	1%
Serving Size 1/2 steak (150g)	Saturated Fat 1g	7%	Dietary Fiber <1g	4%
Servings per Recipe 4	Cholesterol 44mg	15%	Sugars 3g	
Calories 165	Sodium 179mg	7%	Protein 23g	
Calories from Fat 53	Vitamin A 8% • Vitamin C 25% • Calcium 2% • Iron 8%			

*Percent Daily Values (DV) are based on a 2000 calorie diet.

Menu Planning Guide

One serving of this recipe provides:

1 Meat, Poultry & Fish
1/2 Vegetable

Diet Exchanges:

3 lean meat • 1/2 vegetable

Tuna Steaks with Red Pepper Sauce

Serve with Grilled Yellow Squash & Zucchini Fans (p 108)
and Savory Wild Rice (p 97)

2 large red peppers
2 teaspoons snipped fresh basil leaves
½ teaspoon pepper, divided
¼ teaspoon salt
4 bluefin tuna steaks (4 oz. each), 1 inch thick
½ teaspoon olive oil
   Fresh lemon juice

4 servings

1 Place red peppers on baking sheet. Place under broiler with surface of peppers 1 to 2 inches from heat. Broil for 11 to 15 minutes, or until peppers blister and blacken, turning peppers frequently. Remove from heat. Place peppers in paper or plastic bag. Seal bag. Let stand for 10 minutes. Peel and seed peppers. Finely chop 1 pepper. Set aside.

2 Process second pepper in blender or food processor until almost smooth. In serving dish, combine processed pepper, chopped pepper, basil, ¼ teaspoon pepper and the salt. Cover to keep warm.

3 Meanwhile, spray rack in broiler pan with nonstick vegetable cooking spray. Arrange steaks on prepared rack. Brush evenly with oil. Sprinkle evenly with remaining ¼ teaspoon pepper. Place under broiler with surface of steaks 4 to 5 inches from heat. Broil for 10 to 14 minutes, or until fish is firm and just begins to flake, turning steaks over once. Sprinkle steaks with lemon juice. Serve sauce with steaks.

Grilling tip: Prepare as directed in steps 1 and 2. Spray cooking grid with nonstick vegetable cooking spray. Prepare grill for medium direct heat. Brush steaks evenly with oil and sprinkle evenly with remaining ¼ teaspoon pepper. Place steaks on grid. Grill, covered, for 6 to 8 minutes, or until fish is firm and just begins to flake, turning steaks over once. Continue as directed.

Nutrition Facts	Amount/serving	%DV*	Amount/serving	%DV*
Serving Size 1 steak with sauce (131g)	Total Fat 2g	3%	Total Carbohydrate 3g	1%
	Saturated Fat <1g	2%	Dietary Fiber <1g	3%
Servings per Recipe 4	Cholesterol 52mg	17%	Sugars 2g	
Calories 140 Calories from Fat 15	Sodium 176mg	7%	Protein 27g	

Vitamin A 30% • Vitamin C 110% • Calcium 2% • Iron 6%
*Percent Daily Values (DV) are based on a 2000 calorie diet.

Menu Planning Guide
One serving of this recipe provides:
 1 Meat, Poultry & Fish
 ½ Vegetable

Diet Exchanges:
3 lean meat • ½ vegetable

Broiled Vegetable Ratatouille

Serve with a crusty French roll and a crisp green salad

1 medium eggplant (1 lb.), cut into 1-inch slices

1 large red pepper, cut in half lengthwise and seeded

1 small zucchini squash (5 oz.), cut in half lengthwise

2 tablespoons olive oil, divided

½ cup water

2 medium carrots, sliced (1 cup)

2 cups small broccoli flowerets

1½ cups thickly sliced mushrooms

1 can (8 oz.) tomato sauce

1 tablespoon snipped fresh parsley

1 teaspoon dried summer savory

¼ teaspoon pepper

6 servings

1 Arrange eggplant slices, red pepper halves and zucchini halves on rack in broiler pan. Brush vegetables evenly with 1 tablespoon oil. Place under broiler with surface of vegetables 4 to 5 inches from heat. Broil for 10 to 12 minutes, or until vegetables are browned and tender-crisp, turning vegetables over once and brushing with remaining 1 tablespoon oil. Cool slightly. Coarsely chop vegetables. Heat oven to 350°F.

2 Meanwhile, bring water to boil in 2-quart saucepan over high heat. Add carrots. Cover. Reduce heat to medium. Cook for 2 to 3 minutes, or until carrots are tender-crisp. Stir in broccoli and mushrooms. Re-cover. Cook for 2 to 2½ minutes, or until color of broccoli brightens. Remove from heat. Drain.

3 Combine chopped vegetables, carrot mixture and remaining ingredients in 13 x 9-inch baking dish. Cover with foil. Bake for 20 to 25 minutes, or until vegetables are tender and edges are bubbly.

Nutrition Facts	Amount/serving	%DV*	Amount/serving	%DV*
Serving Size 1 cup (236g)	Total Fat 6g	7%	Total Carbohydrate 14g	4%
Servings per Recipe 6	Saturated Fat 1g	3%	Dietary Fiber 6g	22%
Calories 106	Cholesterol 0mg	0%	Sugars 6g	
Calories from Fat 46	Sodium 262mg	10%	Protein 4g	

Vitamin A 160% • Vitamin C 120% • Calcium 4% • Iron 12%

*Percent Daily Values (DV) are based on a 2000 calorie diet.

Menu Planning Guide
One serving of this recipe provides:

3 Vegetable

Diet Exchanges:
3 vegetable

Broiled Vegetable Sandwiches

Serve with French Lentil Salad (p 73) or Tomato-Basil Soup (p 105)

3 tablespoons plain nonfat or low-fat yogurt

2 tablespoons low-fat or nonfat mayonnaise

1 tablespoon snipped fresh basil

1 teaspoon spicy brown mustard

1 small eggplant (12 oz.), cut into 1/4-inch
    slices

1 medium zucchini, cut diagonally into
    1/4-inch slices (1 cup)

1 small onion, cut into 1/4-inch slices (1 cup)

1 cup red pepper slices (1/2-inch slices)

1 tablespoon olive oil

1 fresh baguette (8 oz.), 20 inches long

1/2 cup shredded part-skim or nonfat
    mozzarella cheese

4 servings

1 Combine yogurt, mayonnaise, basil and mustard in small mixing bowl. Set dressing aside.

2 Spray rack in broiler pan with nonstick vegetable cooking spray. Arrange eggplant, zucchini, onion and red pepper slices in single layer on rack. Brush lightly with oil. Place under broiler with surface of vegetables 4 to 5 inches from heat. Broil for 14 to 18 minutes, or until golden brown, turning vegetables over once. Set aside.

3 Cut baguette in half lengthwise. Place baguette halves, cut side up, on baking sheet. Place under broiler with surface of bread 4 to 5 inches from heat. Broil for 1 to 2 minutes, or until golden brown. Spread dressing evenly on baguette halves. Layer vegetables on bottom half of baguette. Top with cheese.

4 Place bottom half of baguette under broiler with surface of cheese 4 to 5 inches from heat. Broil for 30 seconds to 1 minute, or until cheese is melted. Place top half of baguette over cheese. Slice evenly into 4 sandwiches.

Nutrition Facts	Amount/serving	%DV*	Amount/serving	%DV*
Serving Size 1 sandwich (210g)	Total Fat 6g	10%	Total Carbohydrate 30g	10%
Servings per Recipe 4	Saturated Fat 1g	5%	Dietary Fiber 3g	12%
Calories 213	Cholesterol 3mg	1%	Sugars 7g	
Calories from Fat 57	Sodium 382mg	16%	Protein 10g	

Vitamin A 35% • Vitamin C 90% • Calcium 20% • Iron 8%
*Percent Daily Values (DV) are based on a 2000 calorie diet.

Menu Planning Guide
One serving of this recipe provides:
2 Vegetable
1 Bread, Cereal, Rice & Pasta

Diet Exchanges:
1/2 lean meat • 1 starch • 2 vegetable • 1 fat

Chickpea Burgers

Serve with Double Artichoke Salad (p 69)
or Orzo Pasta (p 93) and Tri-bean Bake (p 106)

½ cup spicy vegetable juice

½ cup water

1 cup uncooked couscous

2 cups canned chickpeas (garbanzo beans),
   rinsed and drained

⅓ cup sesame seed, toasted*

2 tablespoons snipped fresh parsley

2 tablespoons Dijon mustard

2 tablespoons fresh lemon juice

1 tablespoon soy sauce

2 teaspoons dried rosemary leaves

2 cloves garlic, minced

½ teaspoon ground cumin

½ teaspoon salt

¼ teaspoon pepper

¼ cup finely shredded carrot

1 teaspoon olive oil, divided

4 whole wheat pitas, cut in half (optional)

16 thin slices tomato (optional)
   Leaf lettuce (optional)
   Prepared mustard (optional)

8 servings

To toast sesame seed, cook in a dry skillet over medium-low heat, stirring frequently to prevent burning.

1 Combine vegetable juice and water in 1-quart saucepan. Bring to simmer over high heat. Stir in couscous. Remove from heat. Cover. Let stand for 5 minutes.

2 Combine chickpeas and sesame seed in food processor. Process until coarsely ground. Add couscous, parsley, Dijon mustard, lemon juice, soy sauce, rosemary, garlic, cumin, salt and pepper. Process until smooth. Stir in carrot.

3 Shape mixture into eight ½-inch-thick patties. Prepare grill for medium direct heat. Spray cooking grid with nonstick vegetable cooking spray. Brush patties evenly with ½ teaspoon oil. Place patties oil-side-down on prepared grid. Grill, covered, for 4 to 5½ minutes, or until browned on bottom.

4 Brush tops of burgers evenly with remaining ½ teaspoon oil. Turn burgers over. Grill, covered, for 4 to 5 minutes, or until browned on other side. Place one burger in each pita half. Stuff pitas evenly with tomato slices and lettuce. Top with prepared mustard. Serve immediately.

Nutrition Facts	Amount/serving	%DV*	Amount/serving	%DV*	Menu Planning Guide
Serving Size 1 burger (159g)	Total Fat 5g	7%	Total Carbohydrate 29g	10%	One serving of this recipe provides:
Servings per Recipe 8	Saturated Fat 1g	3%	Dietary Fiber 4g	17%	1 Bread, Cereal, Rice & Pasta
Calories 185	Cholesterol 0mg	0%	Sugars 3g		
Calories from Fat 45	Sodium 510mg	21%	Protein 7g		
	Vitamin A 25% • Vitamin C 15% • Calcium 4% • Iron 10%				**Diet Exchanges:**
	*Percent Daily Values (DV) are based on a 2000 calorie diet.				2 starch • ½ fat

Open-face Bagel Melts

Serve with Tomato-Basil Soup (p 105)
or Lemon Broccoli & Cauliflower Salad (p 77)

1 medium onion, sliced and separated into
   rings
1/2 cup green pepper strips (2 x 1/4-inch strips)
1/2 cup yellow pepper strips (2 x 1/4-inch
   strips)
1 tablespoon snipped fresh watercress
   or basil leaves
1 clove garlic, minced
2 teaspoons prepared horseradish
2 plain bagels, cut in half, toasted
8 slices tomato
4 oz. reduced-fat Monterey Jack cheese,
   cut into 12 strips (2¼ x 1 x 1/4-inch
   strips)

4 servings

1 Spray 10-inch nonstick skillet with non-stick vegetable cooking spray. Heat skillet over medium heat. Add onion, pepper strips, watercress and garlic. Cook for 5 to 6 minutes, or until vegetables are tender-crisp, stirring constantly. Remove from heat. Cover to keep warm. Set aside.

2 Spread horseradish evenly on bagel halves. Arrange 2 slices tomato and 3 strips cheese on each bagel half. Place bagels on rack in broiler pan.

3 Place bagels under broiler with surface of cheese 3 to 5 inches from heat. Broil for 2 to 3½ minutes, or until cheese is melted. Top bagels evenly with onion mixture before serving.

Nutrition Facts	Amount/serving	%DV*	Amount/serving	%DV*
Serving Size 1 sandwich (163g)	Total Fat 6g	9%	Total Carbohydrate 25g	8%
	Saturated Fat 3g	15%	Dietary Fiber 2g	8%
Servings per Recipe 4	Cholesterol 20mg	7%	Sugars 4g	
Calories 204 Calories from Fat 52	Sodium 409mg	17%	Protein 14g	
	Vitamin A 15% • Vitamin C 90% • Calcium 30% • Iron 10%			
	*Percent Daily Values (DV) are based on a 2000 calorie diet.			

Menu Planning Guide
One serving of this recipe provides:
1/2 Milk, Yogurt & Cheese
 1 Vegetable
 1 Bread, Cereal, Rice & Pasta

Diet Exchanges:
1 medium-fat meat • 1 starch • 1 vegetable

Black Bean & Mango Salad

Serve with Rum-spiced Pork Chops (p 27) or Halibut Vera Cruz (p 45)

Dressing:

¼ cup snipped fresh mint leaves

2 tablespoons fresh lime juice

2 tablespoons ready-to-serve chicken broth

1 tablespoon olive oil

1 teaspoon ground coriander

1 teaspoon sugar

⅛ teaspoon ground nutmeg

2 cans (15 oz. each) black beans, rinsed and
  drained

⅓ cup sliced green onions

6 lettuce leaves

2 kiwifruit, peeled and sliced

1 mango, peeled and sliced
  Fresh mint leaves (optional)

6 servings

1 Combine dressing ingredients in medium mixing bowl. Whisk to dissolve sugar. Add beans. Toss to coat. Cover with plastic wrap. Let stand at room temperature for 1 hour, stirring occasionally.

2 Stir in green onions. To serve, line 6 serving plates with lettuce. Spoon about ½ cup bean mixture onto center of each lettuce leaf. Arrange kiwifruit and mango slices around bean mixture. Garnish with fresh mint leaves, if desired.

Nutrition Facts	Amount/serving	%DV*	Amount/serving	%DV*	Menu Planning Guide
Serving Size approximately ½ cup (222g)	Total Fat 3g	5%	Total Carbohydrate 37g	12%	One serving of this recipe provides:
	Saturated Fat <1g	2%	Dietary Fiber 11g	43%	½ Meat, Poultry & Fish
Servings per Recipe 6	Cholesterol 0mg	0%	Sugars 11g		½ Fruit
Calories 198 Calories from Fat 30	Sodium 211mg	9%	Protein 11g		

Vitamin A 30% • Vitamin C 60% • Calcium 6% • Iron 15%

*Percent Daily Values (DV) are based on a 2000 calorie diet.

Diet Exchanges:
2 starch • ½ fruit

Confetti Cabbage Slaw

Serve with Chicken Kabobs with Poppy Seed Baste (p 35) or Herbed Flank Steak Sandwiches (p 20)

3/4 cup plain nonfat or low-fat yogurt

1/4 cup sugar

3 tablespoons white vinegar

1/8 teaspoon white pepper

1 bag (16 oz.) prepared cabbage slaw mix

1 can (8 oz.) crushed pineapple in juice, drained

1/4 cup finely chopped red pepper

2 tablespoons sliced green onion

12 servings

1 Combine yogurt, sugar, vinegar and white pepper in 2-cup measure. Stir until sugar is dissolved. In large mixing bowl or salad bowl, combine yogurt mixture, slaw mix, pineapple, red pepper and onion. Toss to combine. Cover with plastic wrap. Chill at least 2 hours to blend flavors, stirring occasionally. Stir before serving. Serve with slotted spoon.

Nutrition Facts	Amount/serving	%DV*	Amount/serving	%DV*
Serving Size approximately 1/2 cup (81g)	Total Fat <1g	0%	Total Carbohydrate 10g	3%
	Saturated Fat <1g	0%	Dietary Fiber 1g	4%
Servings per Recipe 12	Cholesterol <1mg	0%	Sugars 9g	
Calories 44 Calories from Fat 2	Sodium 18mg	1%	Protein 2g	

Vitamin A 4% • Vitamin C 35% • Calcium 6% • Iron 2%
*Percent Daily Values (DV) are based on a 2000 calorie diet.

Menu Planning Guide

One serving of this recipe provides:

1/2 Vegetable

Diet Exchanges:

1/2 starch • 1/2 vegetable

Creamy Horseradish Dressing†

Serve over green salad with Beef Eye Round Steaks with Vegetables (p 11) or Fresh Tuna Burgers (p 43)

1/4 *cup nonfat or reduced-fat mayonnaise*
1/4 *cup fresh orange juice*
1/4 *cup white vinegar*
2 *teaspoons honey*
2 *teaspoons Dijon mustard*
2 *teaspoons prepared horseradish*

1 cup

1 Combine all ingredients in small mixing bowl. Whisk to blend.

Variations:

Cucumber-Dill Dressing

1 *cup finely chopped seeded peeled cucumber, drained on paper towels*
1/3 *cup low-fat or nonfat buttermilk*
2 *tablespoons nonfat or reduced-fat mayonaise*
2 *teaspoons fresh lemon juice*
1/2 *teaspoon dried dill weed*
1/2 *teaspoon sugar*
1/4 *teaspoon dry mustard*

1 cup

1 Prepare dressing as directed above.

Citrus Ginger Dressing

1/4 *teaspoon grated ruby red grapefruit peel (optional)*
1/2 *cup fresh ruby red grapefruit juice*
2 *teaspoons vegetable oil*
1 *green onion, finely chopped*
1 *clove garlic, minced*
1 *teaspoon grated fresh gingerroot*
1/8 *teaspoon pepper*

About 1/2 cup

1 Prepare dressing as directed at left. Cover with plastic wrap. Chill several hours or overnight to allow flavors to blend.

†Nutrition Facts	Amount/serving	%DV*	Amount/serving	%DV*	Menu Planning Guide
Serving Size 2 tablespoons (27g)	Total Fat <1g	0%	Total Carbohydrate 4g	1%	One serving of this recipe provides:
Servings per Recipe 8	Saturated Fat 0g	0%	Dietary Fiber 0g	0%	
Calories 17	Cholesterol 0mg	0%	Sugars 3g		
Calories from Fat 1	Sodium 117mg	5%	Protein 0g		
	Vitamin A 0% • Vitamin C 6% • Calcium 0% • Iron 0%				Diet Exchanges: free
	*Percent Daily Values (DV) are based on a 2000 calorie diet.				

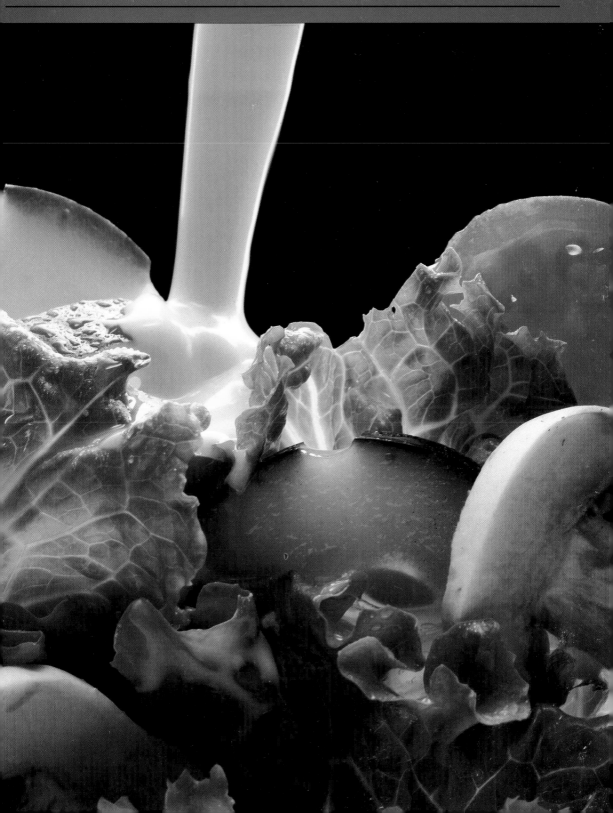

Double Artichoke Salad

Serve with Broiled Fruited Pork Chops (p 14)
or Chickpea Burgers (p 59)

1 can (14 oz.) artichoke hearts in water,
    drained (reserve 1/4 cup liquid), divided
2 tablespoons olive oil
1 tablespoon tarragon vinegar
1 tablespoon chopped onion
1 teaspoon Dijon mustard
1 clove garlic, minced
1/4 to 1/2 teaspoon freshly ground pepper
6 cups torn fresh romaine lettuce
1 cup red pepper strips (2 x 1/8-inch strips)
1 cup nonfat shredded Cheddar cheese

8 servings

1 Place half of artichokes, the reserved liquid, the oil, vinegar, onion, mustard, garlic and ground pepper in food processor or blender. Process until smooth. Cover dressing with plastic wrap. Chill.

2 Cut remaining artichokes into quarters. In large mixing bowl or salad bowl, combine artichokes, lettuce, pepper strips and cheese. Toss to combine. Serve salad with dressing.

Nutrition Facts	Amount/serving	%DV*	Amount/serving	%DV*
Serving Size 1 cup salad with dressing (119g)	Total Fat 4g	5%	Total Carbohydrate 3g	1%
	Saturated Fat 1g	3%	Dietary Fiber 1g	5%
Servings per Recipe 8	Cholesterol 3mg	1%	Sugars 1g	
Calories 65	Sodium 164mg	7%	Protein 6g	
Calories from Fat 32	Vitamin A 45% • Vitamin C 60% • Calcium 15% • Iron 6%			

*Percent Daily Values (DV) are based on a 2000 calorie diet.

Menu Planning Guide
One serving of this recipe provides:
1 Vegetable

Diet Exchanges:
1/2 lean meat • 1/2 fat

Fennel & Orange Salad

Serve with Fresh Tuna Burgers (p 43)
or Herbed Cornish Game Hens (p 36)

¼ cup fresh orange juice
1½ teaspoons rice wine vinegar
⅛ teaspoon sugar
⅛ teaspoon freshly ground pepper
3 medium seedless oranges
6 cups torn fresh lettuce leaves

1 cup thinly sliced fennel bulb
2 tablespoons chopped walnuts
  Candied ginger, finely chopped (optional)

6 servings

1 Combine juice, vinegar, sugar and pepper in 1-cup measure. Set dressing aside.

2 Remove peel and white membrane from oranges with sharp knife. Hold fruit over medium mixing bowl to catch juice.

3 Cut to center between fruit segments and divide membranes, releasing fruit into bowl.

4 Combine oranges, lettuce, fennel and walnuts in large salad bowl or mixing bowl. Whisk dressing with fork until well blended. Pour dressing over orange mixture. Toss to coat. Garnish salad with ginger. Serve immediately.

Nutrition Facts	Amount/serving	%DV*	Amount/serving	%DV*
Serving Size 1 cup (150g) Servings per Recipe 6 Calories 64 Calories from Fat 16	Total Fat 2g	3%	Total Carbohydrate 12g	4%
	Saturated Fat <1g	1%	Dietary Fiber 3g	12%
	Cholesterol 0mg	0%	Sugars 8g	
	Sodium 13mg	1%	Protein 2g	
	Vitamin A 8% • Vitamin C 70% • Calcium 4% • Iron 4%			
	*Percent Daily Values (DV) are based on a 2000 calorie diet.			

Menu Planning Guide

One serving of this recipe provides:
1 Vegetable
½ Fruit

Diet Exchanges:
½ fruit • ½ fat

French Lentil Salad

Serve with Broiled Vegetable Sandwiches (p 56)
or Salmon Croquettes (p 49)

5 cups plus ¼ cup water, divided
1½ cups brown lentils, rinsed and drained
1 large shallot, halved
¼ teaspoon salt
½ cup finely chopped onion
½ cup finely chopped celery
½ cup finely chopped carrot
2 cloves garlic, minced

Dressing:

¼ cup balsamic vinegar
2 tablespoons olive oil
1 teaspoon sugar
½ teaspoon dried thyme leaves
½ teaspoon coarsely ground pepper

   Crumbled chèvre (goat cheese) (optional)
   Snipped fresh parsley (optional)

10 servings

1 Bring 5 cups water to boil in 3-quart saucepan over high heat. Add lentils and shallot. Return to boil. Reduce heat to low. Cover. Simmer for 20 to 25 minutes, or until lentils are tender but not mushy. Drain. Remove and discard shallot. Place lentils in large mixing bowl. Blot with paper towels to remove excess moisture. Stir in salt. Set aside.

2 Combine remaining ¼ cup water, the onion, celery, carrot and garlic in 10-inch nonstick skillet. Cook over medium heat for 5 to 9 minutes, or until vegetables are tender-crisp and water is boiled off, stirring occasionally.

3 Add vegetable mixture to lentils. In 1-cup measure, combine dressing ingredients. Add to lentil mixture. Toss to combine. Cover with plastic wrap. Chill at least 2 hours. Serve on lettuce-lined plates. Top with chèvre and parsley.

Nutrition Facts	Amount/serving	%DV*	Amount/serving	%DV*
Serving Size ½ cup (110g)	Total Fat 3g	5%	Total Carbohydrate 18g	6%
Servings per Recipe 10	Saturated Fat 0g	0%	Dietary Fiber 7g	27%
Calories 131	Cholesterol 0mg	0%	Sugars 4g	
Calories from Fat 27	Sodium 66mg	3%	Protein 7g	

Vitamin A 35% • Vitamin C 6% • Calcium 2% • Iron 15%
*Percent Daily Values (DV) are based on a 2000 calorie diet.

Menu Planning Guide

One serving of this recipe provides:
½ Meat, Poultry & Fish
½ Vegetable

Diet Exchanges:

1 starch • ½ vegetable • ½ fat

Greek Salad

Serve with Greek Burgers (p 17) or as a main dish with a crusty roll

Dressing:

1/4 cup crumbled feta cheese

2 tablespoons fresh lemon juice

2 teaspoons olive oil

1 tablespoon grated red onion with juice

1/2 teaspoon dried dill weed

1/2 teaspoon dried oregano leaves

1/4 teaspoon pepper

4 cups coarsely torn romaine lettuce

1 cup sliced cucumber

1/2 cup thinly sliced red onion

2 Roma tomatoes, quartered

2 pepperoncini peppers, sliced into thin rings
(optional)

8 pitted Kalamata olives, slivered (optional)

6 servings

1 Combine dressing ingredients in large mixing bowl. Add romaine. Toss well to coat each leaf. Add cucumber and sliced onion. Toss to combine.

2 Arrange salad on serving platter or individual serving plates. Garnish with tomatoes, peppers and olives.

Nutrition Facts	Amount/serving	%DV*	Amount/serving	%DV*
Serving Size 1 cup (107g)	Total Fat 4g	6%	Total Carbohydrate 5g	2%
Servings per Recipe 6	Saturated Fat 2g	9%	Dietary Fiber 1g	6%
Calories 61	Cholesterol 9mg	3%	Sugars 3g	
Calories from Fat 35	Sodium 120mg	5%	Protein 3g	

Vitamin A 25% • Vitamin C 30% • Calcium 8% • Iron 4%

*Percent Daily Values (DV) are based on a 2000 calorie diet.

Menu Planning Guide

One serving of this recipe provides:

1 Vegetable

Diet Exchanges:

1 vegetable • 1/2 fat

Lemon Broccoli & Cauliflower Salad

Serve with Herbed Flank Steak Sandwiches (p 20)
or Open-face Bagel Melts (p 61)

4 *cups small fresh broccoli flowerets*

2 *cups small fresh cauliflowerets*

1/2 *cup water*

3/4 *cup shredded carrot*

2 *tablespoons chopped red onion*

2 *tablespoons raisins*

1 *tablespoon shelled sunflower seeds*

Dressing:

1/3 *cup nonfat mayonnaise*

2 *tablespoons plain nonfat or low-fat yogurt*

2 *teaspoons honey*

1/2 *teaspoon grated lemon peel*

12 servings

1 Combine broccoli, cauliflower and water in 3-quart saucepan. Cover. Bring to boil over medium-high heat. Cook for 4 to 5 minutes, or just until color brightens, stirring occasionally. Drain.

2 Combine broccoli, cauliflower, carrot, onion, raisins and seeds in large mixing bowl. Cover with plastic wrap. Chill at least 2 hours. In small mixing bowl, combine dressing ingredients. Add to vegetable mixture. Toss to coat. Serve immediately.

Nutrition Facts	Amount/serving	%DV*	Amount/serving	%DV*
Serving Size 1/2 cup (69g)	Total Fat 1g	1%	Total Carbohydrate 7g	2%
Servings per Recipe 12	Saturated Fat 0g	0%	Dietary Fiber 2g	8%
Calories 35	Cholesterol 0mg	0%	Sugars 4g	
Calories from Fat 5	Sodium 90mg	4%	Protein 2g	

Vitamin A 45% • Vitamin C 50% • Calcium 2% • Iron 2%

*Percent Daily Values (DV) are based on a 2000 calorie diet.

Menu Planning Guide
One serving of this recipe provides:

1 Vegetable

Diet Exchanges:
1 vegetable

Spicy Apple Slaw

*Serve with Honey-Mustard Chops & Carrots (p 23)
or Fresh Tuna Burgers (p 43)*

Dressing:

1/2 cup plain nonfat or low-fat yogurt
2 tablespoons orange juice
2 tablespoons sugar
1/2 teaspoon ground cinnamon
1/8 teaspoon ground nutmeg

2 medium Rome apples, cored and
   coarsely chopped (2 cups)
1 1/2 cups shredded green cabbage
1 cup shredded red cabbage
1 medium Granny Smith apple, cored and
   coarsely chopped (1 cup)
2 tablespoons chopped walnuts (optional)
1 tablespoon dried currants

10 servings

1 Combine dressing ingredients in 1-cup measure. Stir to dissolve sugar. Set aside. In large mixing bowl or salad bowl, combine remaining ingredients. Pour dressing over apple mixture. Toss to combine. Chill 30 minutes before serving.

Nutrition Facts	Amount/serving	%DV*	Amount/serving	%DV*
Serving Size 1/2 cup (69g)	Total Fat 0g	0%	Total Carbohydrate 11g	4%
Servings per Recipe 10	Saturated Fat 0g	0%	Dietary Fiber 1g	6%
Calories 45	Cholesterol 0mg	0%	Sugars 9g	
Calories from Fat 2	Sodium 12mg	1%	Protein 1g	

Vitamin A 0% • Vitamin C 20% • Calcium 4% • Iron 2%
*Percent Daily Values (DV) are based on a 2000 calorie diet.

Menu Planning Guide
One serving of this recipe provides:
1 Fruit
1/2 Vegetable

Diet Exchanges:
1 fruit

Tabbouleh Salad

Serve with Rosemary Butterflied Leg of Lamb (p 24) or Greek Burgers (p 17)

2 cups boiling water

1 cup uncooked bulgur (cracked wheat)

1 medium tomato, seeded and finely chopped
    (1 cup)

1 cup snipped fresh parsley

¼ cup thinly sliced green onions

Dressing:

¼ cup fresh lemon juice

1 tablespoon olive oil

¼ teaspoon salt

¼ teaspoon pepper

10 servings

1 Combine water and bulgur in medium mixing bowl. Let stand for 30 minutes. Drain, pressing with back of spoon to remove excess moisture. In same bowl, combine bulgur, tomato, parsley and onions.

2 Combine dressing ingredients in 1-cup measure. Add dressing to bulgur mixture. Toss to coat. Chill. Serve tabbouleh salad on lettuce-lined plates or in hollowed-out bell pepper halves, if desired.

Nutrition Facts	Amount/serving	%DV*	Amount/serving	%DV*
Serving Size approximately ½ cup (84g)	Total Fat 2g	3%	Total Carbohydrate 13g	4%
	Saturated Fat <1g	1%	Dietary Fiber 3g	12%
Servings per Recipe 10	Cholesterol 0mg	0%	Sugars 1g	
Calories 68	Sodium 62mg	3%	Protein 2g	
Calories from Fat 15	Vitamin A 8% • Vitamin C 25% • Calcium 2% • Iron 4%			
	*Percent Daily Values (DV) are based on a 2000 calorie diet.			

Menu Planning Guide

One serving of this recipe provides:

1 Bread, Cereal, Rice & Pasta

Diet Exchanges:

1 starch

Colorful Marinated Vegetables

Serve with Rosemary Butterflied Leg of Lamb (p 24)
or Herbed Flank Steak Sandwiches (p 20)

3 medium zucchini, cut into ½-inch slices
   (5 cups)

2 medium carrots, cut into ¼-inch slices
   (1 cup)

½ cup thinly sliced onion, separated into
   rings

½ cup coarsely chopped red pepper

½ cup water

¼ cup spicy vegetable juice

2 tablespoons white wine vinegar

2 tablespoons fresh lemon juice

1 tablespoon snipped fresh parsley

1 clove garlic, minced

1 teaspoon sugar

¼ teaspoon celery seed

¼ teaspoon salt

12 servings

1 Combine zucchini, carrots, onion, pepper and water in 3-quart saucepan. Cover. Cook over high heat for 5 to 7 minutes, or until vegetables are tender-crisp, stirring occasionally. Drain. Set aside.

2 Combine remaining ingredients in 1-cup measure. In large mixing bowl or salad bowl, combine vegetable mixture and juice mixture. Toss to coat. Cover with plastic wrap. Chill at least 4 hours, stirring occasionally. Serve with slotted spoon.

Nutrition Facts	Amount/serving	%DV*	Amount/serving	%DV*
Serving Size approximately ½ cup (61g)	Total Fat <1g	0%	Total Carbohydrate 4g	1%
	Saturated Fat <1g	0%	Dietary Fiber 1g	4%
Servings per Recipe 12	Cholesterol 0mg	0%	Sugars 2g	
Calories 15 Calories from Fat 1	Sodium 69mg	3%	Protein 1g	

Vitamin A 45% • Vitamin C 25% • Calcium 2% • Iron 2%
*Percent Daily Values (DV) are based on a 2000 calorie diet.

Menu Planning Guide
One serving of this recipe provides:
1 Vegetable

Diet Exchanges:
1 vegetable

Corn & Leek Pudding

Serve with Brandy Pepper Steaks (p 12) or Honey-Mustard Chops & Carrots (p 23)

1 teaspoon margarine or butter

1 small leek, thinly sliced (1 cup)

1 pkg. (10 oz.) frozen corn, defrosted, divided

½ cup skim milk

½ cup frozen cholesterol-free egg product, defrosted, or 2 eggs

½ teaspoon dry mustard

¼ teaspoon salt

¼ teaspoon freshly ground pepper

⅓ cup crushed low-sodium soda crackers

2 teaspoons margarine or butter, melted

6 servings

1 Heat oven to 350°F. Spray 8-inch square baking dish with nonstick vegetable cooking spray. Set aside. In 10-inch nonstick skillet, melt 1 teaspoon margarine over medium heat. Add leek. Cook for 3 to 5 minutes, or until leek is tender, stirring frequently. Spread leek and half of corn in bottom of prepared dish. Set aside.

2 Combine remaining corn, the milk, egg product, mustard, salt and pepper in food processor or blender. Process until corn is creamed. Pour processed corn mixture over corn and leek in dish.

3 Combine crackers and melted margarine in small mixing bowl. Sprinkle evenly over corn mixture. Bake for 40 to 45 minutes, or until pudding is set and topping is golden brown.

Nutrition Facts	Amount/serving	%DV*	Amount/serving	%DV*
Serving Size ½ cup (108g)	Total Fat 3g	4%	Total Carbohydrate 15g	5%
Servings per Recipe 6	Saturated Fat 1g	3%	Dietary Fiber 2g	7%
Calories 92	Cholesterol 0mg	0%	Sugars 2g	
Calories from Fat 23	Sodium 182mg	8%	Protein 5g	

Vitamin A 8% • Vitamin C 4% • Calcium 4% • Iron 6%

*Percent Daily Values (DV) are based on a 2000 calorie diet.

Menu Planning Guide

One serving of this recipe provides:

1 Vegetable

Diet Exchanges:

1 starch

Dixie Vegetable Dish

Serve with Swordfish with Creole Relish (p 51) or Cajun Chicken Divan (p 32)

1 can (16 oz.) black-eyed peas, rinsed and drained

1 pkg. (10 oz.) frozen corn, defrosted

1 medium tomato, seeded and chopped (1 cup)

1 small zucchini, cut lengthwise into quarters, then sliced crosswise (1 cup)

¼ cup water

1½ teaspoons snipped fresh basil leaves or ½ teaspoon dried basil leaves

¼ teaspoon salt

6 servings

1 Combine all ingredients in 2-quart saucepan. Cover. Cook over high heat for 5 to 7 minutes, or until vegetables are hot and flavors are blended, stirring occasionally. Drain.

Nutrition Facts	Amount/serving	%DV*	Amount/serving	%DV*
Serving Size approximately ½ cup (164g) Servings per Recipe 6	Total Fat <1g	0%	Total Carbohydrate 24g	8%
	Saturated Fat <1g	0%	Dietary Fiber 5g	20%
Calories 108	Cholesterol 0mg	0%	Sugars 4g	
Calories from Fat 3	Sodium 97mg	4%	Protein 4g	

Vitamin A 15% • Vitamin C 15% • Calcium 10% • Iron 6%

*Percent Daily Values (DV) are based on a 2000 calorie diet.

Menu Planning Guide
One serving of this recipe provides:

1 Vegetable

Diet Exchanges:
1½ starch

Garlic Green Beans

Serve with Salmon Croquettes (p 49) or Greek Pork Tenderloin (p 18)

8 oz. fresh green beans, cut lengthwise into
   thin strips

3/4 cup water

1/2 cup chopped seeded tomato

1/4 cup chopped red onion

2 tablespoons sugar

2 tablespoons tarragon vinegar

2 tablespoons fresh lemon juice

3 cloves garlic, minced

1/4 teaspoon salt

1/8 teaspoon coarsely ground pepper

4 servings

1 Combine beans and water in 2-quart saucepan. Cover. Cook over high heat for 5 to 6 minutes, or until beans are tender-crisp, stirring occasionally. Drain.

2 Combine beans and remaining ingredients in medium mixing bowl or salad bowl. Cover with plastic wrap. Chill at least 2 hours to blend flavors, stirring occasionally. Serve with slotted spoon.

Nutrition Facts	Amount/serving	%DV*	Amount/serving	%DV*
Serving Size 1/2 cup (106g) Servings per Recipe 4 Calories 56 Calories from Fat 3	Total Fat 0g	0%	Total Carbohydrate 14g	5%
	Saturated Fat 0g	0%	Dietary Fiber 2g	8%
	Cholesterol 0mg	0%	Sugars 9g	
	Sodium 138mg	6%	Protein 1g	
	Vitamin A 10% • Vitamin C 25% • Calcium 4% • Iron 4%			
	*Percent Daily Values (DV) are based on a 2000 calorie diet.			

Menu Planning Guide

One serving of this recipe provides:

1 Vegetable

Diet Exchanges:

1/2 starch • 1 vegetable

Mexicali Corn on the Cob

Serve with Tequila Turkey (p 39) or Swordfish with Creole Relish (p 51)

¼ cup catsup

2 tablespoons chopped green chilies

½ teaspoon chili powder

¼ teaspoon ground cumin

4 ears fresh corn on the cob (10 to 12 oz. each), in husk

4 servings

1 Combine catsup, chilies, chili powder and cumin in small bowl. Set aside. Gently pull back, but do not detach, corn husks. Remove silks. Soak ears of corn in cold water for 10 minutes. Shake off excess water. Brush catsup mixture evenly on ears of corn.

2 Pull husks up around corn. Gather ends of husks at top of ears and secure with thin pieces of husk or string. Prepare grill for medium direct heat. Grill corn, covered, for 30 to 35 minutes, or until tender, turning ears occasionally.

Nutrition Facts	Amount/serving	%DV*	Amount/serving	%DV*
Serving Size 1 ear (99g)	Total Fat 1g	2%	Total Carbohydrate 24g	8%
Servings per Recipe 4	Saturated Fat <1g	0%	Dietary Fiber 2g	8%
Calories 98	Cholesterol 0mg	0%	Sugars 4g	
Calories from Fat 10	Sodium 142mg	6%	Protein 3g	

Vitamin A 8% • Vitamin C 10% • Calcium 0% • Iron 4%

*Percent Daily Values (DV) are based on a 2000 calorie diet.

Menu Planning Guide

One serving of this recipe provides:

1 Vegetable

Diet Exchanges:

1½ starch

Orzo Pasta

Serve with Greek Pork Tenderloin (p 18), Herbed Cornish Game Hens (p 36) or Chickpea Burgers (p 59)

1 cup uncooked orzo pasta (rosamarina)

1 teaspoon olive oil

1 medium tomato, seeded and chopped (1 cup)

¼ cup finely chopped red onion

1 tablespoon snipped fresh parsley

2 teaspoons balsamic vinegar

½ teaspoon salt

¼ teaspoon coarsely crushed fennel seed

¼ teaspoon freshly ground pepper

6 servings

1 Prepare pasta as directed on package. Drain. In medium salad bowl or mixing bowl, combine pasta and oil. Toss to coat. Add remaining ingredients. Toss to combine. Serve immediately.

Nutrition Facts	Amount/serving	%DV*	Amount/serving	%DV*
Serving Size approximately ½ cup (98g) Servings per Recipe 6	Total Fat 1g	2%	Total Carbohydrate 18g	6%
	Saturated Fat <1g	1%	Dietary Fiber 1g	5%
	Cholesterol 0mg	0%	Sugars 2g	
Calories 99 Calories from Fat 12	Sodium 182mg	8%	Protein 3g	
	Vitamin A 4% • Vitamin C 10% • Calcium 0% • Iron 6%			
	*Percent Daily Values (DV) are based on a 2000 calorie diet.			

Menu Planning Guide

One serving of this recipe provides:

½ Vegetable
1 Bread, Cereal, Rice & Pasta

Diet Exchanges:

1 starch • ½ vegetable

Rosemary New Potatoes & Beans

*Serve with Herbed Flank Steak Sandwiches (p 20)
or Broiled Pesto Halibut Steaks (p 41)*

2　cups water

1　lb. new potatoes, thinly sliced (3 cups)

¼　cup chopped onion

2　teaspoons instant chicken bouillon granules

1　clove garlic, minced

1　can (16 oz.) red kidney beans or Great
　　Northern beans, rinsed and drained

¼　cup green pepper strips (2 x ¼-inch strips)

¼　cup red pepper strips (2 x ¼-inch strips)

1　tablespoon olive oil

1　tablespoon red wine vinegar

2　teaspoons dried parsley flakes

¼　teaspoon dried rosemary leaves, crushed

8 servings

1 Place water in 3-quart saucepan. Bring to boil over high heat. Add potatoes, onion, bouillon and garlic. Return to boil. Cover. Reduce heat to low. Cook for 10 to 12 minutes, or until potatoes are tender-crisp. Drain.

2 Add remaining ingredients. Stir to combine. Return to heat. Cook, uncovered, over medium heat for 2 to 3 minutes, or until hot, stirring occasionally. Cover. Let stand for 5 minutes before serving.

Nutrition Facts	Amount/serving	%DV*	Amount/serving	%DV*
Serving Size ½ cup (128g) Servings per Recipe 8	Total Fat 2g	3%	Total Carbohydrate 27g	9%
	Saturated Fat <1g	1%	Dietary Fiber 5g	21%
Calories 147	Cholesterol 0mg	0%	Sugars 3g	
Calories from Fat 20	Sodium 223mg	10%	Protein 6g	
	Vitamin A 2% • Vitamin C 35% • Calcium 2% • Iron 15%			
	*Percent Daily Values (DV) are based on a 2000 calorie diet.			

Menu Planning Guide

One serving of this recipe provides:

½　Meat, Poultry & Fish
½　Vegetable

Diet Exchanges:
2 starch

Savory Wild Rice

Serve with Broiled Fruited Pork Chops (p 14) or Tuna Steaks with Red Pepper Sauce (p 53)

4 cups water
¾ cup uncooked wild rice, rinsed and drained
¼ cup uncooked brown rice, rinsed and drained
1 tablespoon instant chicken bouillon granules
1 cup sliced fresh mushrooms
½ cup finely chopped red pepper
1 teaspoon margarine
2 tablespoons thinly sliced green onion
⅛ teaspoon pepper
Snipped fresh parsley

6 servings

1 Combine water, rices and bouillon in 2-quart saucepan. Bring to boil over high heat. Cover. Reduce heat to low. Simmer for 45 to 55 minutes, or until wild rice kernels are open. Drain. Place rice in serving dish. Cover to keep warm. Set aside.

2 Spray 10-inch nonstick skillet with nonstick vegetable cooking spray. Add mushrooms, red pepper and margarine to skillet. Cook over medium heat for 3 to 5 minutes, or until red pepper is tender-crisp, stirring frequently. Add mushroom mixture, onion and pepper to rice. Stir to combine. Sprinkle with parsley.

Microwave tip: Omit margarine. In 1-quart casserole, combine mushrooms and red pepper. Cover. Microwave at High for 1½ to 2 minutes, or until red pepper is tender-crisp, stirring once. Continue as directed.

Nutrition Facts	Amount/serving	%DV*	Amount/serving	%DV*
Serving Size approximately ½ cup (108g) Servings per Recipe 6	Total Fat 1g	2%	Total Carbohydrate 20g	7%
	Saturated Fat <1g	1%	Dietary Fiber 2g	8%
	Cholesterol 0mg	0%	Sugars 1g	
Calories 102 Calories from Fat 10	Sodium 162mg	7%	Protein 3g	

Vitamin A 15% • Vitamin C 35% • Calcium 0% • Iron 4%
*Percent Daily Values (DV) are based on a 2000 calorie diet.

Menu Planning Guide
One serving of this recipe provides:
½ Vegetable
1 Bread, Cereal, Rice & Pasta

Diet Exchanges:
1 starch • ½ vegetable

Seasoned Potato Wedges

*Serve with BBQ Chicken (p 31), Tequila Turkey (p 39)
or Salmon Croquettes (p 49)*

Seasoning:

2 *tablespoons grated Parmesan cheese*

1 *teaspoon paprika*

1/2 *teaspoon poppy seed*

1/2 *teaspoon salt*

1/4 *teaspoon garlic powder*

1/4 *teaspoon pepper*

1/8 *to* 1/4 *teaspoon cayenne*

1/8 *teaspoon celery seed*

6 *russet potatoes (5 to 7 oz. each), scrubbed*

2 *teaspoons vegetable oil*

6 servings

1 Heat oven to 400°F. Spray baking sheet with nonstick vegetable cooking spray. Set aside. In large plastic food-storage bag, combine seasoning ingredients. Set aside.

2 Slice each potato lengthwise into 6 wedges. Rinse wedges under cold water. Pat dry with paper towels. Place wedges in large mixing bowl. Drizzle oil over wedges. Stir to evenly coat. Add wedges to bag with seasoning. Seal bag. Shake to coat. Arrange wedges in single layer on prepared sheet.

3 Bake for 30 to 40 minutes, or until wedges are tender and potato skins are crisp, stirring and turning wedges after half the time.

Nutrition Facts	Amount/serving	%DV*	Amount/serving	%DV*
Serving Size 6 wedges (120g)	Total Fat 2g	4%	Total Carbohydrate 29g	10%
Servings per Recipe 6	Saturated Fat 1g	3%	Dietary Fiber 3g	12%
Calories 151	Cholesterol 2mg	0%	Sugars 2g	
Calories from Fat 22	Sodium 226mg	9%	Protein 4g	

Vitamin A 6% • Vitamin C 25% • Calcium 4% • Iron 10%
*Percent Daily Values (DV) are based on a 2000 calorie diet.

Menu Planning Guide

One serving of this recipe provides:

1 Vegetable

Diet Exchanges:

2 starch

Tangy Lime Risotto

*Serve with Teriyaki Steak & Vegetable Kabobs (p 28),
Tequila Turkey (p 39) or Orange-sauced Roughy (p 47)*

1 cup uncooked arborio rice* or short-grain
    white rice, rinsed and drained
¼ cup chopped onion
2 teaspoons olive oil
3½ cups hot water
1 to 2 tablespoons fresh lime juice
1½ teaspoons instant chicken bouillon granules
1 cup frozen baby peas and mushrooms
¼ cup shredded fresh Parmesan cheese
1 tablespoon snipped fresh parsley

8 servings

* *Arborio rice is traditionally used for risotto
because its high starch content gives the dish its
requisite creamy texture.*

1 Combine rice, onion and oil in 12-inch nonstick skillet. Cook over medium heat for 6 to 8 minutes, or just until rice begins to brown, stirring constantly. Add water, juice and bouillon. Simmer for 20 to 25 minutes, or until rice is tender and water is nearly absorbed, stirring occasionally.

2 Stir in peas and mushrooms, cheese and parsley. Cook for 2½ to 4 minutes, or until peas are hot and texture is creamy, stirring frequently.

Nutrition Facts	Amount/serving	%DV*	Amount/serving	%DV*
Serving Size approximately ½ cup (108g)	Total Fat 2g	4%	Total Carbohydrate 25g	8%
	Saturated Fat <1g	4%	Dietary Fiber 1g	4%
Servings per Recipe 8	Cholesterol 3mg	1%	Sugars 2g	
Calories 141 Calories from Fat 21	Sodium 239mg	10%	Protein 4g	
	Vitamin A 2% • Vitamin C 4% • Calcium 4% • Iron 8%			
	*Percent Daily Values (DV) are based on a 2000 calorie diet.			

Menu Planning Guide

One serving of this recipe provides:
  1 Bread, Cereal, Rice & Pasta

Diet Exchanges:
1½ starch

Three-bean Medley

Serve with BBQ Chicken (p 31) or Honey-Mustard Chops & Carrots (p 23)

Dressing:

- *1/3 cup red wine vinegar*
- *1 tablespoon sugar*
- *1/4 teaspoon instant minced garlic*
- *1/8 teaspoon crushed red pepper flakes*

- *1 pkg. (10 oz.) frozen cut green beans*
- *1 can (15 1/2 oz.) red kidney beans, rinsed and drained*
- *1 can (15 1/2 oz.) butter beans, rinsed and drained*
- *1/2 cup thinly sliced halved red onion*

10 servings

1 Combine dressing ingredients in 1-cup measure. Set aside. Prepare green beans as directed on package. Drain. Place green beans in large mixing bowl. Stir in kidney beans, butter beans and onion. Add dressing. Toss to coat. Cover with plastic wrap. Chill at least 2 hours to blend flavors, stirring occasionally.

Nutrition Facts	Amount/serving	%DV*	Amount/serving	%DV*
Serving Size approximately 1/2 cup (117g) Servings per Recipe 10 Calories 114 Calories from Fat 6	Total Fat 1g	1%	Total Carbohydrate 21g	7%
	Saturated Fat 0g	0%	Dietary Fiber 5g	20%
	Cholesterol 0mg	0%	Sugars 3g	
	Sodium 192mg	8%	Protein 7g	

Vitamin A 2% • Vitamin C 6% • Calcium 4% • Iron 10%
*Percent Daily Values (DV) are based on a 2000 calorie diet.

Menu Planning Guide
One serving of this recipe provides:
1/2 Meat, Poultry & Fish

Diet Exchanges:
1 1/2 starch

Tomato-Basil Soup

*Serve with Open-face Bagel Melts (p 61)
or Broiled Vegetable Sandwiches (p 56)*

1/3 cup chopped shallots

 1 clove garlic, minced

 1 teaspoon olive oil

 1 can (28 oz.) Roma tomatoes, undrained
     and cut up

1/2 cup water

1/4 cup snipped fresh basil leaves

1/2 teaspoon instant chicken bouillon granules

1/2 teaspoon sugar

1/2 teaspoon freshly ground pepper

 4 fresh Roma tomatoes, chopped (2 cups),
     divided

 1 cup skim milk, divided

6 servings

1 Combine shallots, garlic and oil in 2-quart saucepan. Cook over medium heat for 3 to 3½ minutes, or until tender, stirring frequently. Add canned tomatoes, water, basil, bouillon, sugar and pepper. Cook for 5½ to 8 minutes, or until mixture is hot and flavors are blended, stirring occasionally. Remove from heat.

2 Combine half of tomato mixture, 2 Roma tomatoes and ½ cup milk in food processor or blender. Process until smooth. Set purée aside. Repeat with remaining ingredients. Return purée to saucepan. Cook over medium heat for 8 to 10 minutes, or until soup is hot, stirring occasionally.

3 Spoon into serving dishes. Top each serving with 1 crostini*, if desired.

To make crostini, arrange 6 thin slices of toasted Italian bread on baking sheet. Brush slices evenly with 1 tablespoon olive oil. Top each with 2 thin slices fresh Roma tomato, 1 small fresh basil leaf and 1 teaspoon shredded fresh Parmesan cheese. Broil 5 inches from heat for 4 to 5 minutes, or until golden brown.

Nutrition Facts	Amount/serving	%DV*	Amount/serving	%DV*
Serving Size approximately 1 cup (247g)	Total Fat 1g	2%	Total Carbohydrate 12g	4%
Servings per Recipe 6	Saturated Fat 0g	0%	Dietary Fiber 2g	8%
Calories 66	Cholesterol <1mg	0%	Sugars 7g	
Calories from Fat 12	Sodium 317mg	13%	Protein 3g	

Vitamin A 45% • Vitamin C 50% • Calcium 10% • Iron 6%
*Percent Daily Values (DV) are based on a 2000 calorie diet.

Menu Planning Guide
One serving of this recipe provides:
2 Vegetable

Diet Exchanges:
2 vegetable

Tri-bean Bake

Serve with Honey-Mustard Chops & Carrots (p 23)
or Chickpea Burgers (p 59)

1 medium onion, thinly sliced (1 cup)
1 stalk celery, thinly sliced (½ cup)
1 teaspoon vegetable oil
1 can (16 oz.) pinto beans, rinsed and drained
1 can (15 oz.) butter beans, rinsed and drained
1 can (15 oz.) garbanzo beans, rinsed and
   drained
1 can (8 oz.) tomato sauce
¼ cup frozen apple juice concentrate, defrosted
1 tablespoon light molasses (optional)
½ teaspoon dry mustard

10 servings

1 Heat oven to 375°F. In 10-inch nonstick skillet, combine onion, celery and oil. Cook over medium heat for 5 to 8 minutes, or until vegetables are tender, stirring occasionally.

2 Stir in remaining ingredients. Spoon mixture into 2-quart casserole. Cover. Bake for 25 to 30 minutes, or until hot and bubbly.

Nutrition Facts	Amount/serving	%DV*	Amount/serving	%DV*
	Total Fat 2g	3%	Total Carbohydrate 34g	11%
Serving Size approximately 1 cup (168g)	Saturated Fat <1g	1%	Dietary Fiber 9g	36%
Servings per Recipe 10	Cholesterol 0mg	0%	Sugars 7g	
Calories 182 Calories from Fat 17	Sodium 241mg	10%	Protein 9g	

Vitamin A 4% • Vitamin C 15% • Calcium 6% • Iron 15%
*Percent Daily Values (DV) are based on a 2000 calorie diet.

Menu Planning Guide
One serving of this recipe provides:
½ Meat, Poultry & Fish

Diet Exchanges:
2½ starch

Grilled Yellow Squash & Zucchini Fans

Serve with Fresh Tuna Burgers (p 43), BBQ Chicken (p 31), or Tuna Steaks with Red Pepper Sauce (p 53)

2 medium yellow squash (8 oz. each)
2 medium zucchini squash (8 oz. each)

¼ cup fat-free Italian dressing

4 servings

1 Prepare grill for medium direct heat. Spray cooking grid with nonstick vegetable cooking spray. Starting 1 inch from stem end of each squash, cut lengthwise into ¼-inch strips, leaving strips attached to stem end.

2 Arrange squash on cooking grid, pressing to fan out. Grill, covered, for 12 to 15 minutes, or until squash is tender-crisp, turning over and basting with dressing twice. Sprinkle each serving with shredded fresh Parmesan cheese, if desired.

Nutrition Facts	Amount/serving	%DV*	Amount/serving	%DV*
Serving Size 1 squash (230g)	Total Fat 1g	1%	Total Carbohydrate 9g	3%
Servings per Recipe 4	Saturated Fat <1g	1%	Dietary Fiber 3g	12%
Calories 43	Cholesterol 0mg	0%	Sugars 5g	
Calories from Fat 5	Sodium 214mg	9%	Protein 2g	

Vitamin A 15% • Vitamin C 25% • Calcium 4% • Iron 4%
*Percent Daily Values (DV) are based on a 2000 calorie diet.

Menu Planning Guide
One serving of this recipe provides:
2 Vegetable

Diet Exchanges:
2 vegetable